JUANITA BYNUM

Morning Glory

Meditation Scriptures

Pneuma Life

PUBLISHING

Morning Glory Meditation Scriptures

Copyright © 1999 by Juanita Bynum

ISBN 1-56229-158-0

Pneuma Life Publishing
4451 Parliament Place
Lanham, MD 20706
301-577-4052
http://www.pneumalife.com

Printed in the United States of America

Meditation Scriptures

INTRODUCTION

*G*od is calling you to commune with Him early in the morning. Embrace the call and all that God seeks to impart unto you. When you open your eyes in the morning, connect to the beauty of His holiness. Before you speak to another, why don't you speak to the Lord first? Commune with Him and enter into His presence. Allow the Lord to penetrate your spirit and get locked into your thoughts.

I know firsthand that committing to early morning prayer and worship will challenge most-just like it challenged me. But understand something, its rewards will take you to a new level in God. Nobody said that it would be easy—great things usually aren't. Biblical history teaches us that most of the great acts in the Bible were wrought when? In the morning.

The majority of today's Christians are stuck in mediocrity and are satisfied to do just enough to get by rather than doing what it takes to propel themselves to a greater level in God. It's time to stop playing games and step out of your comfort zone. If you're not challenged, if your life isn't changing for the better, and if you're not growing in the Lord, then you're just wasting your time. God knows that giving up that last bit of sleep will be a press for most of us. Yet, He also knows that when you're after something from Him, you will persevere. Your sacrifice will not be in vain.

Early in the morning, you're fresh. Before your children get up, before you're entrenched in the cares of this world, hear what the Spirit of the Lord wants to say to you. Give God the first fruits of your mind before your spouse gets it, before your children get it, before your boss gets it, and before the bill collectors get it. Offer it unto the Lord. Then, when the world hits you and the fire of your trial comes, it cannot shake the Word that the Lord spoke to you early that morning. That Word is your manna from heaven. It will sustain you through anything you'll face that day.

Yesterday's prayer won't do. Today's manna is waiting. Yesterday's Word won't be enough to sustain you. Tomorrow has it's own troubles, new levels and new devils. So everyday you need a fresh Word. Get up early and let the Word be the first thing that hits your spirit. Commit yourself to early morning worship. Press on to your next spiritual level. Up, up, up. Follow His lead, for He is your Bright and Morning Star. Rise up and bask in His Presence . . . bask in the Morning Glory.

Meditation Scriptures

TABLE OF CONTENTS

Meditation Scriptures

PRAISE

I will praise the Lord according to his righteousness: and will sing praise to the name of the Lord most high. Psalm 7:17

And now shal l mine head be lifted up above mine enemies round about me: therefore will I offer in his tabernacle sacrifices of joy; I will sing, yea, I will sing praises unto the Lord. Psalm 27:6

The Lord is my strength and my shield; my heart trusted in him, and I am helped: therefore my heart greatly rejoiceth; and with my song will I praise him. Psalm 28:7

Rejoice in the Lord, O ye righteous: for praise is comely for the upright. Praise the Lord with harp: sing unto him with the psaltery and an instrument of ten strings. Psalm 33:1-2

I will bless the Lord at all times: his praise shall continually be in my mouth. Psalm 34:1

And my tongue shall speak of thy righteousness and of thy praise all the day long. Psalm 35:28

Then will I go unto the altar of God, unto God my exceeding joy: yea, upon the harp will I praise thee, O God my God. Psalm 43:4

In God we boast all the day long, and praise thy name for ever. Selah. Psalm 44:8

Great is the Lord, and greatly to be praised in the city of our God, in the mountain of his holiness. Psalm 48:1

According to thy name, O God, so is thy praise unto the ends of the earth: thy right hand is full of righteousness. Psalm 48:10

O Lord, open thou my lips; and my mouth shall shew forth thy praise. Psalm 51:15

I will praise thee for ever, because thou hast done it: and I will wait on thy name; for it is good before thy saints. Psalm 52:9

In God I will praise his word, in God I have put my trust; I will not fear what flesh can do unto me. Psalm 56:4

In God will I praise his word: in the Lord will I praise his word. Psalm 56:10

My heart is fixed, O God, my heart is fixed: I will sing and give praise. Psalm 57:7

So will I sing praise unto thy name for ever, that I may daily perform my vows. Psalm 61:8

Because thy lovingkindness is better than life, my lips shall praise thee. Psalm 63:3

Make a joyful noise unto God, all ye lands: Sing forth the honour of his name: make his praise glorious. Psalm 66:1-2

O bless our God, ye people, and make the voice of his praise to be heard. Psalm 66:8

Let the people praise thee, O God; let all the people praise thee. Psalm 67:3

Sing unto God, ye kingdoms of the earth; O sing praises unto the Lord; Selah. Psalm 68:32

I will praise the name of God with a song, and will magnify him with thanksgiving. Psalm 69:30

Let the heaven and earth praise him, the seas, and everything that moveth therein. Psalm 69:34

Let my mouth be filled with thy praise and with thy honour all the day. Psalm 71:8

But I will hope continually, and will yet praise thee more and more. Psalm 71:14

I will praise thee, O Lord my God, with all my heart: and I will glorify thy name for evermore. Psalm 86:12

And the heavens shall praise thy wonders, O Lord: thy faithfulness also in the congregation of the saints. Psalm 89:5

It is a good thing to give thanks unto the Lord, and to sing praises unto thy name, O most High: To shew forth thy lovingkindness in the morning, and thy faithfulness every night, Upon an instrument of ten strings, and upon the psaltery; upon the harp with a solemn sound. For the Lord is great, and greatly to be praised: he is to be feared above all gods. Psalm 92:1-4

Make a joyful noise unto the Lord, all the earth: make a loud noise, and rejoice, and sing praise. Psalm 98:4

Make a joyful noise unto the Lord, all ye lands. Serve the Lord with gladness: come before his presence with singing. Psalm 100:1-2

Enter into his gates with thanksgiving, and into his courts with praise: be thankful unto him, and bless his name. For the Lord is good; his mercy is everlasting; and his truth endureth to all generations. Psalm 100:4-5

Then believed they his words; they sang his praise. Psalm 106:12

Oh that men would praise the Lord for his goodness, and for his wonderful works to the children of men! Psalm 107:8

O God, my heart is fixed; I will sing and give praise, even with my glory. Awake, psaltery and harp: I myself will awake early. I will praise thee, O Lord, among the people: and I will sing praises unto thee among the nations. Psalm 108:1-3

Praise ye the Lord. I will praise the Lord with my whole heart, in the assembly of the upright, and in the congregation. Psalm 111:1

Praise ye the Lord. Praise, O ye servants of the Lord, praise the name of the Lord. Blessed be the name of the Lord from this time forth and for evermore. From the rising of the sun unto the going down of the same the Lord's name is to be praised. Psalm 113:1-3

O praise the Lord, all ye nations: praise him, all ye people. For his merciful kindness is great toward us: and the truth of the Lord endureth for ever. Praise ye the Lord. Psalm 117:1-2

Thou art my God, and I will praise thee: thou art my God, I will exalt thee. O give thanks unto the Lord; for he is good: for his mercy endureth for ever. Psalm 118:28-29

I will praise thee with uprightness of heart, when I shall have learned thy righteous judgments. Psalm 119:7

Seven times a day do I praise thee because of thy righteous judgments. Psalm 119:164

Praise the Lord; for the Lord is good: sing praises unto his name; for it is pleasant. Psalm 135:3

I will praise thee with my whole heart: before the gods will I sing praise unto thee. I will worship toward thy holy temple, and praise thy name for thy lovingkindness and for thy truth: for thou hast magnified thy word above all thy name. Psalm 138:1-2

All the kings of the earth shall praise thee, O Lord, when they hear the words of thy mouth. Psalm 138:4

Great is the Lord, and greatly to be praised; and his greatness is unsearchable. Psalm 145:3

Praise ye the Lord: for it is good to sing praises unto our God; for it is pleasant; and praise is comely. Psalm 147:1

Praise ye the Lord. Praise ye the Lord from the heavens: praise him in the heights. Praise ye him, all his angels: praise ye him, all his hosts. Praise ye him, sun and moon: praise him, all ye stars of light. Praise him, ye heavens of heavens, and ye waters that be above the heavens. Let them praise the name of the Lord: for he commanded, and they were created. He hath also stablished them for ever and ever: he hath made a decree which shall not pass. Praise the Lord from the earth, ye dragons, and all deeps: Fire, and hail; snow, and vapour; stormy wind fulfilling his word: Mountains, and all hills; fruitful trees, and all cedars: Beasts, and all cattle; creeping things, and flying fowl: Kings of the earth, and all people; princes, and all judges of the earth: Both young men, and maidens; old men, and children: Let them praise the name of the Lord: for his name alone is excellent; his glory is above the earth and heaven. Psalm 148:1-13

Let the saints be joyful in glory: let them sing aloud upon their beds. Let the high praises of God be in their mouth, and a twoedged sword in their hand. Psalm 149:5-6

Praise ye the Lord. Praise God in his sanctuary: praise him in the firmament of his power. Praise him for his mighty acts: praise him according to his excellent greatness. Praise him with the sound of the trumpet: praise him with the psaltery and harp. Praise him with the timbrel and dance: praise him with stringed instruments and organs. Praise him upon the loud cymbals: praise him upon the high sounding cymbals. Let every thing that hath breath praise the Lord. Praise ye the Lord. Psalm 150:1-6

O Lord, thou art my God; I will exalt thee, I will praise thy name; for thou hast done wonderful things; thy counsels of old are faithfulness and truth. Isaiah 25:1

To appoint unto them that mourn in Zion, to give unto them beauty for ashes, the oil of joy for mourning, the garment of praise for the spirit of heaviness; that they might be called trees of righteousness, the planting of the Lord, that he might be glorified. Isaiah 61:3

And said unto him, Hearest thou what these say? And Jesus saith unto them, Yea; have ye never read, Out of the mouth of babes and sucklings thou hast perfected praise? Matthew 21:16

Saying, Blessed be the King that cometh in the name of the Lord: peace in heaven, and glory in the highest. Luke 19:38

By him therefore let us offer the sacrifice of praise to God continually, that is, the fruit of our lips giving thanks to his name. Hebrews 13:15

And a voice came out of the throne, saying, Praise our God, all ye his servants, and ye that fear him, both small and great. Revelation 19:5

WORSHIP

For thou shalt worship no other god: for the Lord, whose name is Jealous, is a jealous God. Exodus 34:14

Thou, even thou, art Lord alone; thou hast made heaven, the heaven of heavens, with all their host, the earth, and all things that are therein, the seas, and all that is therein, and thou preservest them all; and the host of heaven worshippeth thee. Nehemiah 9:6

All the ends of the world shall remember and turn unto the Lord: and all the kindreds of the nations shall worship before thee. Psalm 22:27

Give unto the Lord the glory due unto his name; worship the Lord in the beauty of holiness. Psalm 29:2

So shall the king greatly desire thy beauty: for he is thy Lord; and worship thou him. Psalm 45:11

All the earth shall worship thee, and shall sing unto thee; they shall sing to thy name. Selah. Psalm 66:4

All nations whom thou hast made shall come and worship before thee, O Lord; and shall glorify thy name. Psalm 86:9

O come, let us worship and bow down: let us kneel before the Lord our maker. Psalm 95:6

Exalt ye the Lord our God, and worship at his footstool; for he is holy. Psalm 99:5

Exalt the Lord our God, and worship at his holy hill; for the Lord our God is holy. Psalm 99:9

We will go into his tabernacles: we will worship at his footstool. Psalm 132:7

I will worship toward thy holy temple, and praise thy name for thy lovingkindness and for thy truth: for thou hast magnified thy word above all thy name. Psalm 138:2

Saying, Where is he that is born King of the Jews? for we have seen his star in the east, and are come to worship him. Matthew 2:2

Then saith Jesus unto him, Get thee hence, Satan: for it is written, Thou shalt worship the Lord thy God, and him only shalt thou serve. Matthew 4:10

And as they went to tell his disciples, behold, Jesus met them, saying, All hail. And they came and held him by the feet, and worshipped him. Matthew 28:9

And when they saw him, they worshipped him: but some doubted. Matthew 28:17

But when he saw Jesus afar off, he ran and worshipped him. Mark 5:6

But the hour cometh, and now is, when the true worshippers shall worship the Father in spirit and in truth: for the Father seeketh such to worship him. God is a Spirit: and they that worship him must worship him in spirit and in truth. John 4:23-24

Now we know that God heareth not sinners: but if any man be a worshipper of God, and doeth his will, him he heareth. John 9:31

For we are the circumcision, which worship God in the spirit, and rejoice in Christ Jesus, and have no confidence in the flesh. Philippians 3:3

The four and twenty elders fall down before him that sat on the throne, and worship him that liveth for ever and ever, and cast their crowns before the throne, saying, Thou art worthy, O Lord, to receive glory and honour and power: for thou hast created all things, and for thy pleasure they are and were created. Revelation 4:10-11

And the four beasts said, Amen. And the four and twenty elders fell down and worshipped him that liveth for ever and ever. Revelation 5:14

And all the angels stood round about the throne, and about the elders and the four beasts, and fell before the throne on their faces, and worshipped God, Saying, Amen: Blessing, and glory, and wisdom, and thanksgiving, and honour, and power, and might, be unto our God for ever and ever. Amen. Revelation 7:11-12

And the four and twenty elders, which sat before God on their seats, fell upon their faces, and worshipped God. Revelation 11:16

Saying with a loud voice, Fear God, and give glory to him; for the hour of his judgment is come: and worship him that made heaven, and earth, and the sea, and the fountains of waters. Revelation 14:7

Meditation Scriptures

Meditation Scriptures

PEACE

And, having made peace through the blood of his cross, by him to reconcile all things unto himself; by him, I say, whether they be things in earth, or things in heaven. Colossians 1:20

I will both lay me down in peace, and sleep: for thou, Lord, only makest me dwell in safety. Psalm 4:8

The Lord will give strength unto his people; the Lord will bless his people with peace. Psalm 29:11

Mark the perfect man, and behold the upright: for the end of that man is peace. Psalm 37:37

He hath delivered my soul in peace from the battle that was against me: for there were many with me. Psalm 55:18

In his days shall the righteous flourish; and abundance of peace so long as the moon endureth. Psalm 72:7

Lord, thou wilt ordain peace for us: for thou also hast wrought all our works in us. Isaiah 26:12

For ye shall go out with joy, and be led forth with peace: the mountains and the hills shall break forth before you into singing, and all the trees of the field shall clap their hands. Isaiah 55:12

He shall enter into peace: they shall rest in their beds, each one walking in his uprightness. Isaiah 57:2

To give light to them that sit in darkness and in the shadow of death, to guide our feet into the way of peace. Luke 1:79

Now the God of hope fill you with all joy and peace in believing, that ye may abound in hope, through the power of the Holy Ghost. Romans 15:13

For God is not the author of confusion, but of peace, as in all churches of the saints. 1 Corinthians 14:33

And let the peace of God rule in your hearts, to the which also ye are called in one body; and be ye thankful. Colossians 3:15

Now the Lord of peace himself give you peace always by all means. The Lord be with you all. 2 Thessalonians 3:16

But now in Christ Jesus ye who sometimes were far off are made nigh by the blood of Christ. For he is our peace, who hath made both one, and hath broken down the middle wall of partition between us. Having abolished in his flesh the enmity, even the law of commandments contained in ordinances; for to make in himself of twain one new man, so making peace. Ephesians 2:13-15

Therefore being justified by faith, we have peace with God through our Lord Jesus Christ. Romans 5:1

Peace I leave with you, my peace I give unto you: not as the world giveth, give I unto you. Let not your heart be troubled, neither let it be afraid. John 14:27

These things I have spoken unto you, that in me ye might have peace. In the world ye shall have tribulation: but be of good cheer; I have overcome the world. John 16:33

Then said Jesus to them again, Peace be unto you: as my Father hath sent me, even so send I you. John 20:21

My son, forget not my law; but let thine heart keep my commandments: For length of days, and long life, and peace, shall they add to thee. Proverbs 3:1-2

Great peace have they which love thy law: and nothing shall offend them. Psalm 119:165

And all thy children shall be taught of the Lord; and great shall be the peace of thy children. Isaiah 54:13

Let us therefore follow after the things which make for peace, and things wherewith one may edify another. Romans 14:19

And as many as walk according to this rule, peace be on them, and mercy, and upon the Israel of God. Galatians 6:16

Be careful for nothing; but in every thing by prayer and supplication with thanksgiving let your requests be made known unto God. And the peace of God, which passeth all understanding, shall keep your hearts and minds through Christ Jesus. Finally, brethren, whatsoever things are true, whatsoever things are honest, whatsoever things are just, whatsoever things are pure, whatsoever things are lovely, whatsoever things are of good report; if there be any virtue, and if there be any praise, think on these things. Those things, which ye have both learned, and received, and heard, and seen in me, do: and the God of peace shall be with you. Philippians 4:6-9

Grace and peace be multiplied unto you through the knowledge of God, and of Jesus our Lord. 2 Peter 1:2

When a man's ways please the Lord, he maketh even his enemies to be at peace with him. Proverbs 16:7

For to be carnally minded is death; but to be spiritually minded is life and peace. Romans 8:6

Thou wilt keep him in perfect peace, whose mind is stayed on thee: because he trusteth in thee. Isaiah 26:3

For the kingdom of God is not meat and drink; but righteousness, and peace, and joy in the Holy Ghost. For he that in these things serveth Christ is acceptable to God, and approved of men. Let us therefore follow after the things which make for peace, and things wherewith one may edify another. Romans 14:17-19

And the work of righteousness shall be peace; and the effect of righteousness quietness and assurance for ever. Isaiah 32:17

Meditation Scriptures

COMFORT

I, even I, am he that comforteth you: who art thou, that thou shouldest be afraid of a man that shall die, and of the son of man which shall be made as grass. Isaiah 51:12

To proclaim the acceptable year of the Lord, and the day of vengeance of our God; to comfort all that mourn. Isaiah 61:2

As one whom his mother comforteth, so will I comfort you; and ye shall be comforted in Jerusalem. Isaiah 66:13

Blessed are they that mourn: for they shall be comforted. Matthew 5:4

And I will pray the Father, and he shall give you another Comforter, that he may abide with you for ever. John 14:16

Blessed be God, even the Father of our Lord Jesus Christ, the Father of mercies, and the God of all comfort; Who comforteth us in all our tribulation, that we may be able to comfort them which are in any trouble, by the comfort wherewith we ourselves are comforted of God. For as the sufferings of Christ abound in us, so our consolation also aboundeth by Christ. 2 Corinthians 1:3-5

Great is my boldness of speech toward you, great is my glorying of you: I am filled with comfort, I am exceeding joyful in all our tribulation. 2 Corinthians 7:4

Nevertheless God, that comforteth those that are cast down, comforted us by the coming of Titus; And not by his coming only, but by the consolation wherewith he was comforted in you, when he told us your earnest desire, your mourning, your fervent mind toward me; so that I rejoiced the more. 2 Corinthians 7:6-7

Finally, brethren, farewell. Be perfect, be of good comfort, be of one mind, live in peace; and the God of love and peace shall be with you. 2 Corinthians 13:11

Comfort your hearts, and stablish you in every good word and work. 2 Thessalonians 2:17

Meditation Scriptures

THE WILL OF GOD

For whosoever shall do the will of God, the same is my brother, and my sister, and mother. Mark 3:35

For whosoever shall do the will of my Father which is in heaven, the same is my brother, and sister, and mother. Matthew 12:50

And it came to pass, when he was in a certain city, behold a man full of leprosy: who seeing Jesus fell on his face, and besought him, saying, Lord, if thou wilt, thou canst make me clean. Luke 5:12

And that servant, which knew his lord's will, and prepared not himself, neither did according to his will, shall be beaten with many stripes. Luke 12:47

If any man will do his will, he shall know of the doctrine, whether it be of God, or whether I speak of myself. John 7:17

Now we know that God heareth not sinners: but if any man be a worshipper of God, and doeth his will, him he heareth. John 9:31

Not with eyeservice, as menpleasers; but as the servants of Christ, doing the will of God from the heart. Ephesians 6:6

For ye have need of patience, that, after ye have done the will of God, ye might receive the promise. Hebrews 10:36

And the world passeth away, and the lust thereof: but he that doeth the will of God abideth for ever. 1 John 2:17

And this is the confidence that we have in him, that, if we ask any thing according to his will, he heareth us: And if we know that he hear us, whatsoever we ask, we know that we have the petitions that we desired of him. 1 John 5:14-15

But I know, that even now, whatsoever thou wilt ask of God, God will give it thee. John 11:22

And he that searcheth the hearts knoweth what is the mind of the Spirit, because he maketh intercession for the saints according to the will of God. Romans 8:27

And he went a little further, and fell on his face, and prayed, saying, O my Father, if it be possible, let this cup pass from me: nevertheless not as I will, but as thou wilt. Matthew 26:39

Thy kingdom come. Thy will be done in earth, as it is in heaven. Matthew 6:10

And he said to them all, If any man will come after me, let him deny himself, and take up his cross daily, and follow me. Luke 9:23

Making request, if by any means now at length I might have a prosperous journey by the will of God to come unto you. Romans 1:10

And be not conformed to this world: but be ye transformed by the renewing of your mind, that ye may prove what is that good, and acceptable, and perfect, will of God. Romans 12:2

And this they did, not as we hoped, but first gave their own selves to the Lord, and unto us by the will of God. 2 Corinthians 8:5

Who gave himself for our sins, that he might deliver us from this present evil world, according to the will of God and our Father: Galatians 1:4

For it is God which worketh in you both to will and to do of his good pleasure. Philippians 2:13

Epaphras, who is one of you, a servant of Christ, saluteth you, always labouring fervently for you in prayers, that ye may stand perfect and complete in all the will of God. Colossians 4:12

Paul, an apostle of Jesus Christ by the will of God, according to the promise of life which is in Christ Jesus. 2 Timothy 1:1

For this is the will of God, even your sanctification, that ye should abstain from fornication. 1 Thessalonians 4:3

Rejoice evermore. Pray without ceasing. In every thing give thanks: for this is the will of God in Christ Jesus concerning you. 1 Thessalonians 5:16-18

For so is the will of God, that with well doing ye may put to silence the ignorance of foolish men: 1 Peter 2:15

That he no longer should live the rest of his time in the flesh to the lusts of men, but to the will of God. 1 Peter 4:2

Wherefore let them that suffer according to the will of God commit the keeping of their souls to him in well doing, as unto a faithful Creator. 1 Peter 4:19

The Lord is not slack concerning his promise, as some men count slackness; but is longsuffering to us-ward, not willing that any should perish, but that all should come to repentance. 2 Peter 3:9

But I know, that even now, whatsoever thou wilt ask of God, God will give it thee. John 11:22

And Jesus answered and said unto him, What wilt thou that I should do unto thee? The blind man said unto him, Lord, that I might receive my sight. And Jesus said unto him, Go thy way; thy faith hath made thee whole. And immediately he received his sight, and followed Jesus in the way. Mark 10:51-52

Wherein God, willing more abundantly to shew unto the heirs of promise the immutability of his counsel, confirmed it by an oath. Hebrews 6:17

The Lord is not slack concerning his promise, as some men count slackness; but is longsuffering to us-ward, not willing that any should perish, but that all should come to repentance. 2 Peter 3:9

Meditation Scriptures

SEEKING GOD

Morning Glory

If my people, which are called by my name, shall humble themselves, and pray, and seek my face, and turn from their wicked ways; then will I hear from heaven, and will forgive their sin, and will heal their land. 2 Chronicles 7:14

I would seek unto God, and unto God would I commit my cause. Job 5:8

And they that know thy name will put their trust in thee: for thou, Lord, hast not forsaken them that seek thee. Psalm 9:10

When thou saidst, Seek ye my face; my heart said unto thee, Thy face, Lord, will I seek. Psalm 27:8

God looked down from heaven upon the children of men, to see if there were any that did understand, that did seek God. Psalm 53:2

The humble shall see this, and be glad: and your heart shall live that seek God. Psalm 69:32

But it is good for me to draw near to God: I have put my trust in the Lord God, that I may declare all thy works. Psalm 73:28

And I set my face unto the Lord God, to seek by prayer and supplication, with fasting, and sackcloth, and ashes. Daniel 9:3

For thus saith the Lord unto the house of Israel, Seek ye me, and ye shall live. Amos 5:4

Seek him that maketh the seven stars and Orion, and turneth the shadow of death into the morning, and maketh the day dark with night: that calleth for the waters of the sea, and poureth them out upon the face of the earth: The Lord is his name. Amos 5:8

Seek ye the Lord, all ye meek of the earth, which have wrought his

judgment; seek righteousness, seek meekness: it may be ye shall be hid in the day of the Lord's anger. Zephaniah 2:3

Yea, many people and strong nations shall come to seek the Lord of hosts in Jerusalem, and to pray before the Lord. Zechariah 8:22

But seek ye first the kingdom of God, and his righteousness; and all these things shall be added unto you. Matthew 6:33

Ask, and it shall be given you; seek, and ye shall find; knock, and it shall be opened unto you: For every one that asketh receiveth; and he that seeketh findeth; and to him that knocketh it shall be opened. Matthew 7:7-8

And I say unto you, Ask, and it shall be given you; seek, and ye shall find; knock, and it shall be opened unto you. Luke 11:9

For every one that asketh receiveth; and he that seeketh findeth; and to him that knocketh it shall be opened. Luke 11:10

And seek not ye what ye shall eat, or what ye shall drink, neither be ye of doubtful mind. For all these things do the nations of the world seek after: and your Father knoweth that ye have need of these things. But rather seek ye the kingdom of God; and all these things shall be added unto you. Luke 12:29-31

But the hour cometh, and now is, when the true worshippers shall worship the Father in spirit and in truth: for the Father seeketh such to worship him. John 4:23

That they should seek the Lord, if haply they might feel after him, and find him, though he be not far from every one of us. Acts 17:27

If ye then be risen with Christ, seek those things which are above, where Christ sitteth on the right hand of God. Colossians 3:1

For the law made nothing perfect, but the bringing in of a better hope did; by the which we draw nigh unto God. Hebrews 7:19

Draw nigh to God, and he will draw nigh to you. Cleanse your hands, ye sinners; and purify your hearts, ye double minded. James 4:8

But if from thence thou shalt seek the Lord thy God, thou shalt find him, if thou seek him with all thy heart and with all thy soul. Deuteronomy 4:29

Now set your heart and your soul to seek the Lord your God. 1 Chronicles 22:19

And they entered into a covenant to seek the Lord God of their fathers with all their heart and with all their soul. 2 Chronicles 15:12

Blessed are they that keep his testimonies, and that seek him with the whole heart. Psalm 119:2

And ye shall seek me, and find me, when ye shall search for me with all your heart. Jeremiah 29:13

O God, thou art my God; early will I seek thee: my soul thirsteth for thee, my flesh longeth for thee in a dry and thirsty land, where no water is. Psalm 63:1

With my soul have I desired thee in the night; yea, with my spirit within me will I seek thee early: for when thy judgments are in the earth, the inhabitants of the world will learn righteousness. Isaiah 26:9

I will go and return to my place, till they acknowledge their offence, and seek my face: in their affliction they will seek me early. Hosea 5:15

I love them that love me; and those that seek me early shall find me. Proverbs 8:17

Therefore came I forth to meet thee, diligently to seek thy face, and I have found thee. Proverbs 7:15

Glory ye in his holy name: let the heart of them rejoice that seek the Lord. Seek the Lord and his strength, seek his face continually.
1 Chronicles 16:10-11

Seek the Lord, and his strength: seek his face evermore. Psalm 105:4

Seek ye the Lord while he may be found, call ye upon him while he is near. Isaiah 55:6

Yet they seek me daily, and delight to know my ways, as a nation that did righteousness, and forsook not the ordinance of their God: they ask of me the ordinances of justice; they take delight in approaching to God. Isaiah 58:2

But without faith it is impossible to please him: for he that cometh to God must believe that he is, and that he is a rewarder of them that diligently seek him. Hebrews 11:6

The meek shall eat and be satisfied: they shall praise the Lord that seek him: your heart shall live for ever. Psalm 22:26

The young lions do lack, and suffer hunger: but they that seek the Lord shall not want any good thing. Psalm 34:10

Evil men understand not judgment: but they that seek the Lord under-stand all things. Proverbs 28:5

The Lord is good unto them that wait for him, to the soul that seeketh him. Lamentations 3:25

And he did evil, because he prepared not his heart to seek the Lord. 2 Chronicles 12:14

Meditation Scriptures

TRUST

The God of my rock; in him will I trust: he is my shield, and the horn of my salvation, my high tower, and my refuge, my saviour; thou savest me from violence. 2 Samuel 22:3

As for God, his way is perfect; the word of the Lord is tried: he is a buckler to all them that trust in him. 2 Samuel 22:31

Wilt thou trust him, because his strength is great? or wilt thou leave thy labour to him? Job 39:11

Offer the sacrifices of righteousness, and put your trust in the Lord. Psalm 4:5

But let all those that put their trust in thee rejoice: let them ever shout for joy, because thou defendest them: let them also that love thy name be joyful in thee. Psalm 5:11

O Lord my God, in thee do I put my trust: save me from all them that persecute me, and deliver me. Psalm 7:1

And they that know thy name will put their trust in thee: for thou, Lord, hast not forsaken them that seek thee. Psalm 9:10

But I have trusted in thy mercy; my heart shall rejoice in thy salvation. Psalm 13:5

Preserve me, O God: for in thee do I put my trust. Psalm 16:1

The Lord is my rock, and my fortress, and my deliverer; my God, my strength, in whom I will trust; my buckler, and the horn of my salvation, and my high tower. Psalm 18:2

As for God, his way is perfect: the word of the Lord is tried: he is a buckler to all those that trust in him. Psalm 18:30

Judge me, O Lord; for I have walked in mine integrity: I have trusted also in the Lord; therefore I shall not slide. Psalm 26:1

The Lord is my strength and my shield; my heart trusted in him, and I am helped: therefore my heart greatly rejoiceth; and with my song will I praise him. Psalm 28:7

In thee, O Lord, do I put my trust; let me never be ashamed: deliver me in thy righteousness. Psalm 31:1

Many sorrows shall be to the wicked: but he that trusteth in the Lord, mercy shall compass him about. Psalm 32:10

O taste and see that the Lord is good: blessed is the man that trusteth in him. Psalm 34:8

Trust in the Lord, and do good; so shalt thou dwell in the land, and verily thou shalt be fed. Psalm 37:3

Commit thy way unto the Lord; trust also in him; and he shall bring it to pass. Psalm 37:5

Blessed is that man that maketh the Lord his trust, and respecteth not the proud, nor such as turn aside to lies. Psalm 40:4

But I am like a green olive tree in the house of God: I trust in the mercy of God for ever and ever. Psalm 52:8

What time I am afraid, I will trust in thee. Psalm 56:3

Trust in him at all times; ye people, pour out your heart before him: God is a refuge for us. Selah. Psalm 62:8

In thee, O Lord, do I put my trust: let me never be put to confusion. Psalm 71:1

I will say of the Lord, He is my refuge and my fortress: my God; in him will I trust. Psalm 91:2

They that trust in the Lord shall be as mount Zion, which cannot be removed, but abideth for ever. Psalm 125:1

Trust in the Lord with all thine heart; and lean not unto thine own understanding. Proverbs 3:5

Behold, God is my salvation; I will trust, and not be afraid: for the Lord Jehovah is my strength and my song; he also is become my salvation. Isaiah 12:2

Yea, mine own familiar friend, in whom I trusted, which did eat of my bread, hath lifted up his heel against me. Psalm 41:9

It is better to trust in the Lord than to put confidence in man. It is better to trust in the Lord than to put confidence in princes. Psalm 118:8-9

Put not your trust in princes, nor in the son of man, in whom there is no help. Psalm 146:3

Thus saith the Lord; Cursed be the man that trusteth in man, and maketh flesh his arm, and whose heart departeth from the Lord. Jeremiah 17:5

Trust ye not in a friend, put ye not confidence in a guide: keep the doors of thy mouth from her that lieth in thy bosom. Micah 7:5

Some trust in chariots, and some in horses: but we will remember the name of the Lord our God. Psalm 20:7

They that trust in their wealth, and boast themselves in the multitude of their riches. None of them can by any means redeem his brother, nor give to God a ransom for him. For the redemption of their soul is precious, and it ceaseth for ever. That he should still live for ever, and not see corruption. For he seeth that wise men die, likewise the fool and the brutish person perish, and leave their wealth to others. Psalm 49:6-10

Let not him that is deceived trust in vanity: for vanity shall be his recompence. Job 15:31

And the disciples were astonished at his words. But Jesus answereth again, and saith unto them, Children, how hard is it for them that trust in riches to enter into the kingdom of God! Mark 10:24

Charge them that are rich in this world, that they be not highminded, nor trust in uncertain riches, but in the living God, who giveth us richly all things to enjoy. 1 Timothy 6:17

Meditation Scriptures

LOVE

God is love; and he that dwelleth in love dwelleth in God, and God in him. 1 John 4:16

There is no fear in love; but perfect love casteth out fear: because fear hath torment. He that feareth is not made perfect in love. 1 John 4:18

Charity suffereth long, and is kind; charity envieth not; charity vaunteth not itself, is not puffed up, Doth not behave itself unseemly, seeketh not her own, is not easily provoked, thinketh no evil; Rejoiceth not in iniquity, but rejoiceth in the truth; Beareth all things, believeth all things, hopeth all things, endureth all things. Charity never faileth: but whether there be prophecies, they shall fail; whether there be tongues, they shall cease; whether there be knowledge, it shall vanish away. 1 Corinthians 13:4-8

Though I speak with the tongues of men and of angels, and have not charity, I am become as sounding brass, or a tinkling cymbal. And though I have the gift of prophecy, and understand all mysteries, and all knowledge; and though I have all faith, so that I could remove mountains, and have not charity, I am nothing. And though I bestow all my goods to feed the poor, and though I give my body to be burned, and have not charity, it profiteth me nothing. 1 Corinthians 13:1-3

And now abideth faith, hope, charity, these three; but the greatest of these is charity. 1 Corinthians 13:13

The Lord openeth the eyes of the blind: the Lord raiseth them that are bowed down: the Lord loveth the righteous. Psalm 146:8

For as a young man marrieth a virgin, so shall thy sons marry thee: and as the bridegroom rejoiceth over the bride, so shall thy God rejoice over thee. Isaiah 62:5

The Lord hath appeared of old unto me, saying, Yea, I have loved thee with an everlasting love: therefore with lovingkindness have I drawn thee. Jeremiah 31:3

I will heal their backsliding, I will love them freely: for mine anger is turned away from him. Hosea 14:4

For God so loved the world, that he gave his only begotten Son, that whosoever believeth in him should not perish, but have everlasting life. John 3:16

For the Father himself loveth you, because ye have loved me, and have believed that I came out from God. John 16:27

And the glory which thou gavest me I have given them; that they may be one, even as we are one: I in them, and thou in me, that they may be made perfect in one; and that the world may know that thou hast sent me, and hast loved them, as thou hast loved me. John 17:22-23

And I have declared unto them thy name, and will declare it: that the love wherewith thou hast loved me may be in them, and I in them. John 17:26

But God commendeth his love toward us, in that, while we were yet sinners, Christ died for us. Romans 5:8

But God, who is rich in mercy, for his great love wherewith he loved us, Even when we were dead in sins, hath quickened us together with Christ, by grace ye are saved. And hath raised us up together, and made us sit together in heavenly places in Christ Jesus: That in the ages to come he might shew the exceeding riches of his grace in his kindness toward us through Christ Jesus. Ephesians 2:4-7

And to know the love of Christ, which passeth knowledge, that ye might be filled with all the fulness of God. Ephesians 3:19

Now our Lord Jesus Christ himself, and God, even our Father, which hath loved us, and hath given us everlasting consolation and good hope through grace, Comfort your hearts, and stablish you in every good word and work. 2 Thessalonians 2:16-17

Behold, what manner of love the Father hath bestowed upon us, that we should be called the sons of God: therefore the world knoweth us not, because it knew him not. 1 John 3:1

Beloved, let us love one another: for love is of God; and every one that loveth is born of God, and knoweth God. He that loveth not knoweth not God; for God is love. In this was manifested the love of God toward us, because that God sent his only begotten Son into the world, that we might live through him. Herein is love, not that we loved God, but that he loved us, and sent his Son to be the propitiation for our sins. Beloved, if God so loved us, we ought also to love one another. 1 John 4:7-11

And we have known and believed the love that God hath to us. God is love; and he that dwelleth in love dwelleth in God, and God in him. 1 John 4:16

We love him, because he first loved us. 1 John 4:19

But as it is written, Eye hath not seen, nor ear heard, neither have entered into the heart of man, the things which God hath prepared for them that love him. 1 Corinthians 2:9

Know therefore that the Lord thy God, he is God, the faithful God, which keepeth covenant and mercy with them that love him and keep his commandments to a thousand generations. Deuteronomy 7:9

Delight thyself also in the Lord; and he shall give thee the desires of thine heart. Psalm 37:4

Whom have I in heaven but thee? and there is none upon earth that I desire beside thee. Psalm 73:25

Because he hath set his love upon me, therefore will I deliver him: I will set him on high, because he hath known my name. Psalm 91:14

The Lord preserveth all them that love him: but all the wicked will he destroy. Psalm 145:20

I love them that love me; and those that seek me early shall find me. Proverbs 8:17

That I may cause those that love me to inherit substance; and I will fill their treasures. Proverbs 8:21

He that hath my commandments, and keepeth them, he it is that loveth me: and he that loveth me shall be loved of my Father, and I will love him, and will manifest myself to him. John 14:21

Grace be with all them that love our Lord Jesus Christ in sincerity. Amen. Ephesians 6:24

Behold, how good and how pleasant it is for brethren to dwell together in unity! Psalm 133:1

But I say unto you, Love your enemies, bless them that curse you, do good to them that hate you, and pray for them which despitefully use you, and persecute you. Matthew 5:44

Therefore all things whatsoever ye would that men should do to you, do ye even so to them: for this is the law and the prophets. Matthew 7:12

Morning Glory

And thou shalt love the Lord thy God with all thy heart, and with all thy soul, and with all thy mind, and with all thy strength: this is the first commandment. And the second is like, namely this, Thou shalt love thy neighbour as thyself. There is none other commandment greater than these. Mark 12:30-31

This is my commandment, That ye love one another, as I have loved you. Greater love hath no man than this, that a man lay down his life for his friends. John 15:12-13

Be kindly affectioned one to another with brotherly love; in honour preferring one another. Romans 12:10

Love worketh no ill to his neighbour: therefore love is the fulfilling of the law. Romans 13:10

Finally, brethren, farewell. Be perfect, be of good comfort, be of one mind, live in peace; and the God of love and peace shall be with you. 2 Corinthians 13:11

Seeing ye have purified your souls in obeying the truth through the Spirit unto unfeigned love of the brethren, see that ye love one another with a pure heart fervently. 1 Peter 1:22

Finally, be ye all of one mind, having compassion one of another, love as brethren, be pitiful, be courteous: Not rendering evil for evil, or railing for railing: but contrariwise blessing; knowing that ye are thereunto called, that ye should inherit a blessing. 1 Peter 3:8-9

He that loveth his brother abideth in the light, and there is none occasion of stumbling in him. 1 John 2:10

We know that we have passed from death unto life, because we love the brethren. He that loveth not his brother abideth in death. 1 John 3:14

My little children, let us not love in word, neither in tongue; but in deed and in truth. And hereby we know that we are of the truth, and shall assure our hearts before him. 1 John 3:18-19

Beloved, let us love one another: for love is of God; and every one that loveth is born of God, and knoweth God. He that loveth not knoweth not God; for God is love. 1 John 4:7-8

Beloved, if God so loved us, we ought also to love one another. No man hath seen God at any time. If we love one another, God dwelleth in us, and his love is perfected in us. 1 John 4:11-12

If a man say, I love God, and hateth his brother, he is a liar: for he that loveth not his brother whom he hath seen, how can he love God whom he hath not seen? And this commandment have we from him, That he who loveth God love his brother also. 1 John 4:20-21

And now I beseech thee, lady, not as though I wrote a new commandment unto thee, but that which we had from the beginning, that we love one another. 2 John 1:5

Meditation Scriptures

OBEDIENCE

Morning Glory

O that there were such an heart in them, that they would fear me, and keep all my commandments always, that it might be well with them, and with their children for ever! Deuteronomy 5:29

And thou shalt do that which is right and good in the sight of the Lord: that it may be well with thee, and that thou mayest go in and possess the good land which the Lord sware unto thy fathers. Deuteronomy 6:18

Wherefore it shall come to pass, if ye hearken to these judgments, and keep, and do them, that the Lord thy God shall keep unto thee the covenant and the mercy which he sware unto thy fathers.
Deuteronomy 7:12

Keep therefore the words of this covenant, and do them, that ye may prosper in all that ye do. Deuteronomy 29:9

I have set before thee this day life and good, and death and evil; In that I command thee this day to love the Lord thy God, to walk in his ways, and to keep his commandments and his statutes and his judgments, that thou mayest live and multiply: and the Lord thy God shall bless thee in the land whither thou goest to possess it. Deuteronomy 30:15-16

If they obey and serve him, they shall spend their days in prosperity, and their years in pleasures. Job 36:11

Blessed are they that keep judgment, and he that doeth righteousness at all times. Psalm 106:3

So shall I keep thy law continually for ever and ever. Psalm 119:44

I made haste, and delayed not to keep thy commandments. Psalm 119:60

I have refrained my feet from every evil way, that I might keep thy word. Psalm 119:101

Thy testimonies are wonderful: therefore doth my soul keep them.
Psalm 119:129

Wherewithal shall a young man cleanse his way? by taking heed
thereto according to thy word. Psalm 119:9

My son, keep thy father's commandment, and forsake not the law of
thy mother: Bind them continually upon thine heart, and tie them about
thy neck. When thou goest, it shall lead thee; when thou sleepest, it
shall keep thee; and when thou awakest, it shall talk with thee.
Proverbs 6:20-22

Whoso despiseth the word shall be destroyed: but he that feareth the
commandment shall be rewarded. Proverbs 13:13

Whosoever therefore shall break one of these least commandments, and
shall teach men so, he shall be called the least in the kingdom of
heaven: but whosoever shall do and teach them, the same shall be
called great in the kingdom of heaven. Matthew 5:19

Not every one that saith unto me, Lord, Lord, shall enter into the
kingdom of heaven; but he that doeth the will of my Father which is in
heaven. Matthew 7:21

For whosoever shall do the will of my Father which is in heaven, the
same is my brother, and sister, and mother. Matthew 12:50

But Jesus said, Suffer little children, and forbid them not, to come unto
me: for of such is the kingdom of heaven. Matthew 19:14

Verily, verily, I say unto you, He that heareth my word, and believeth
on him that sent me, hath everlasting life, and shall not come into
condemnation; but is passed from death unto life. John 5:24

Verily, verily, I say unto you, If a man keep my saying, he shall never see death. John 8:51

If ye know these things, happy are ye if ye do them. John 13:17

If ye love me, keep my commandments. John 14:15

He that hath my commandments, and keepeth them, he it is that loveth me: and he that loveth me shall be loved of my Father, and I will love him, and will manifest myself to him. John 14:21

Jesus answered and said unto him, If a man love me, he will keep my words: and my Father will love him, and we will come unto him, and make our abode with him. He that loveth me not keepeth not my sayings: and the word which ye hear is not mine, but the Father's which sent me. John 14:23-24

If ye keep my commandments, ye shall abide in my love; even as I have kept my Father's commandments, and abide in his love. John 15:10

Ye are my friends, if ye do whatsoever I command you. John 15:14

Let every soul be subject unto the higher powers. For there is no power but of God: the powers that be are ordained of God. Romans 13:1

Those things, which ye have both learned, and received, and heard, and seen in me, do: and the God of peace shall be with you. Philippians 4:9

And being made perfect, he became the author of eternal salvation unto all them that obey him. Hebrews 5:9

And hereby we do know that we know him, if we keep his command-ments. He that saith, I know him, and keepeth not his commandments, is a liar, and the truth is not in him. But whoso keepeth his word, in him verily is the love of God perfected: hereby know we that we are in him. He that saith he abideth in him ought himself also so to walk, even as he walked. 1 John 2:3-6

And the world passeth away, and the lust thereof: but he that doeth the will of God abideth for ever. 1 John 2:17

And whatsoever we ask, we receive of him, because we keep his commandments, and do those things that are pleasing in his sight. 1 John 3:22

But he said, Yea rather, blessed are they that hear the word of God, and keep it. Luke 11:28

For not the hearers of the law are just before God, but the doers of the law shall be justified. Romans 2:13

Therefore whosoever heareth these sayings of mine, and doeth them, I will liken him unto a wise man, which built his house upon a rock: And the rain descended, and the floods came, and the winds blew, and beat upon that house; and it fell not: for it was founded upon a rock. Matthew 7:24-25

For not the hearers of the law are just before God, but the doers of the law shall be justified. Romans 2:13

But whoso looketh into the perfect law of liberty, and continueth therein, he being not a forgetful hearer, but a doer of the work, this man shall be blessed in his deed. James 1:25

Meditation Scriptures

DIRECTION

Thou wilt shew me the path of life: in thy presence is fulness of joy; at thy right hand there are pleasures for evermore. Psalm 16:11

Shew me thy ways, O Lord; teach me thy paths. Lead me in thy truth, and teach me: for thou art the God of my salvation; on thee do I wait all the day. Psalm 25:4-5

The meek will he guide in judgment: and the meek will he teach his way. All the paths of the Lord are mercy and truth unto such as keep his covenant and his testimonies. Psalm 25:9-10

I will instruct thee and teach thee in the way which thou shalt go: I will guide thee with mine eye. Psalm 32:8

The steps of a good man are ordered by the Lord: and he delighteth in his way. Though he fall, he shall not be utterly cast down: for the Lord upholdeth him with his hand. Psalm 37:23-24

For this God is our God for ever and ever: he will be our guide even unto death. Psalm 48:14

Nevertheless I am continually with thee: thou hast holden me by my right hand. Thou shalt guide me with thy counsel, and afterward receive me to glory. Psalm 73:23-24

So he fed them according to the integrity of his heart; and guided them by the skilfulness of his hands. Psalm 78:72

For he shall give his angels charge over thee, to keep thee in all thy ways. Psalm 91:11

The Lord shall preserve thy going out and thy coming in from this time forth, and even for evermore. Psalm 121:8

The Lord will perfect that which concerneth me: thy mercy, O Lord, endureth for ever: forsake not the works of thine own hands. Psalm 138:8

He keepeth the paths of judgment, and preserveth the way of his saints. Proverbs 2:8

Trust in the Lord with all thine heart; and lean not unto thine own understanding. In all thy ways acknowledge him, and he shall direct thy paths. Proverbs 3:5-6

The integrity of the upright shall guide them: but the perverseness of transgressors shall destroy them. Proverbs 11:3

Without counsel purposes are disappointed: but in the multitude of counsellers they are established. Proverbs 15:22

Commit thy works unto the Lord, and thy thoughts shall be established. Proverbs 16:3

A man's heart deviseth his way: but the Lord directeth his steps. Proverbs 16:9

Man's goings are of the Lord; how can a man then understand his own way? Proverbs 20:24

And many people shall go and say, Come ye, and let us go up to the mountain of the Lord, to the house of the God of Jacob; and he will teach us of his ways, and we will walk in his paths: for out of Zion shall go forth the law, and the word of the Lord from Jerusalem. Isaiah 2:3

For his God doth instruct him to discretion, and doth teach him. Isaiah 28:26

And thine ears shall hear a word behind thee, saying, This is the way, walk ye in it, when ye turn to the right hand, and when ye turn to the left. Isaiah 30:21

And I will bring the blind by a way that they knew not; I will lead them in paths that they have not known: I will make darkness light before them, and crooked things straight. These things will I do unto them, and not forsake them. Isaiah 42:16

I will go before thee, and make the crooked places straight: I will break in pieces the gates of brass, and cut in sunder the bars of iron. Isaiah 45:2

I have raised him up in righteousness, and I will direct all his ways: he shall build my city, and he shall let go my captives, not for price nor reward, saith the Lord of hosts. Isaiah 45:13

Thus saith the Lord, thy Redeemer, the Holy One of Israel; I am the Lord thy God which teacheth thee to profit, which leadeth thee by the way that thou shouldest go. Isaiah 48:17

I have seen his ways, and will heal him: I will lead him also, and restore comforts unto him and to his mourners. Isaiah 57:18

But seek ye first the kingdom of God, and his righteousness; and all these things shall be added unto you. Matthew 6:33

And when he putteth forth his own sheep, he goeth before them, and the sheep follow him: for they know his voice. And a stranger will they not follow, but will flee from him: for they know not the voice of strangers. John 10:4-5

My sheep hear my voice, and I know them, and they follow me.
John 10:27

Howbeit when he, the Spirit of truth, is come, he will guide you into all truth: for he shall not speak of himself; but whatsoever he shall hear, that shall he speak: and he will shew you things to come. John 16:13

This I say then, Walk in the Spirit, and ye shall not fulfil the lust of the flesh. Galatians 5:16

For it is God which worketh in you both to will and to do of his good pleasure. Philippians 2:13

If any of you lack wisdom, let him ask of God, that giveth to all men liberally, and upbraideth not; and it shall be given him. James 1:15

But ye have an unction from the Holy One, and ye know all things.
1 John 2:20

I know thy works: behold, I have set before thee an open door, and no man can shut it: for thou hast a little strength, and hast kept my word, and hast not denied my name. Revelation 3:8

Meditation Scriptures

Hope

Why art thou cast down, O my soul? and why art thou disquieted within me? hope thou in God: for I shall yet praise him, who is the health of my countenance, and my God. Psalm 42:11

Be of good courage, and he shall strengthen your heart, all ye that hope in the Lord. Psalm 31:24

Behold, the eye of the Lord is upon them that fear him, upon them that hope in his mercy. Psalm 33:18

Uphold me according unto thy word, that I may live: and let me not be ashamed of my hope. Psalm 119:116

The Lord taketh pleasure in them that fear him, in those that hope in his mercy. Psalm 147:11

The hope of the righteous shall be gladness: but the expectation of the wicked shall perish. Proverbs 10:28

For to him that is joined to all the living there is hope: for a living dog is better than a dead lion. Ecclesiastes 9:4

Therefore did my heart rejoice, and my tongue was glad; moreover also my flesh shall rest in hope. Acts 2:26

Who against hope believed in hope, that he might become the father of many nations; according to that which was spoken, So shall thy seed be. Romans 4:18

For we are saved by hope: but hope that is seen is not hope: for what a man seeth, why doth he yet hope for? But if we hope for that we see not, then do we with patience wait for it. Romans 8:24-25

Rejoicing in hope; patient in tribulation; continuing instant in prayer. Romans 12:12

Now the God of hope fill you with all joy and peace in believing, that ye may abound in hope, through the power of the Holy Ghost. Romans 15:13

Beareth all things, believeth all things, hopeth all things, endureth all things. 1 Corinthians 13:7

For we through the Spirit wait for the hope of righteousness by faith. Galatians 5:5

The eyes of your understanding being enlightened; that ye may know what is the hope of his calling, and what the riches of the glory of his inheritance in the saints Ephesians 1:18

But let us, who are of the day, be sober, putting on the breastplate of faith and love; and for an helmet, the hope of salvation. 1 Thessalonians 5:8

But Christ as a son over his own house; whose house are we, if we hold fast the confidence and the rejoicing of the hope firm unto the end. Hebrews 3:6

And we desire that every one of you do shew the same diligence to the full assurance of hope unto the end. Hebrews 6:11

That by two immutable things, in which it was impossible for God to lie, we might have a strong consolation, who have fled for refuge to lay hold upon the hope set before us: Which hope we have as an anchor of the soul, both sure and stedfast, and which entereth into that within the veil. Hebrews 6:18-19

For the law made nothing perfect, but the bringing in of a better hope did; by the which we draw nigh unto God. Hebrews 7:19

Blessed be the God and Father of our Lord Jesus Christ, which according to his abundant mercy hath begotten us again unto a lively hope by the resurrection of Jesus Christ from the dead. 1 Peter 1:3

Who by him do believe in God, that raised him up from the dead, and gave him glory; that your faith and hope might be in God. 1 Peter 1:21

Let thy mercy, O Lord, be upon us, according as we hope in thee. Psalm 33:22

For in thee, O Lord, do I hope: thou wilt hear, O Lord my God. Psalm 38:15

And now, Lord, what wait I for? my hope is in thee. Psalm 39:7

Why art thou cast down, O my soul? and why art thou disquieted in me? hope thou in God: for I shall yet praise him for the help of his countenance. Psalm 42:5

Why art thou cast down, O my soul? and why art thou disquieted within me? hope thou in God: for I shall yet praise him, who is the health of my countenance, and my God. Psalm 42:11

For thou art my hope, O Lord God: thou art my trust from my youth. Psalm 71:5

But I will hope continually, and will yet praise thee more and more. Psalm 71:14

That they might set their hope in God, and not forget the works of God, but keep his commandments. Psalm 78:7

Let Israel hope in the Lord: for with the Lord there is mercy, and with him is plenteous redemption. Psalm 130:7

Let Israel hope in the Lord from henceforth and for ever. Psalm 131:3

Happy is he that hath the God of Jacob for his help, whose hope is in the Lord his God. Psalm 146:5

The Lord is my portion, saith my soul; therefore will I hope in him. Lamentations 3:24

It is good that a man should both hope and quietly wait for the salvation of the Lord. Lamentations 3:26

The Lord also shall roar out of Zion, and utter his voice from Jerusalem; and the heavens and the earth shall shake: but the Lord will be the hope of his people, and the strength of the children of Israel. Joel 3:16

And have hope toward God, which they themselves also allow, that there shall be a resurrection of the dead, both of the just and unjust. Acts 24:15

By whom also we have access by faith into this grace wherein we stand, and rejoice in hope of the glory of God. Romans 5:2

Wherefore gird up the loins of your mind, be sober, and hope to the end for the grace that is to be brought unto you at the revelation of Jesus Christ. 1 Peter 1:13

But sanctify the Lord God in your hearts: and be ready always to give an answer to every man that asketh you a reason of the hope that is in you with meekness and fear. 1 Peter 3:15

Remember the word unto thy servant, upon which thou hast caused me to hope. Psalm 119:49

They that fear thee will be glad when they see me; because I have hoped in thy word. Psalm 119:74

My soul fainteth for thy salvation: but I hope in thy word. Psalm 119:81

Thou art my hiding place and my shield: I hope in thy word. Psalm 119:114

I wait for the Lord, my soul doth wait, and in his word do I hope. Psalm 130:5

For whatsoever things were written aforetime were written for our learning, that we through patience and comfort of the scriptures might have hope. Romans 15:4

If ye continue in the faith grounded and settled, and be not moved away from the hope of the gospel, which ye have heard, and which was preached to every creature which is under heaven; whereof I Paul am made a minister. Colossians 1:23

If in this life only we have hope in Christ, we are of all men most miserable. 1 Corinthians 15:19

To whom God would make known what is the riches of the glory of this mystery among the Gentiles; which is Christ in you, the hope of glory. Colossians 1:27

Remembering without ceasing your work of faith, and labour of love, and patience of hope in our Lord Jesus Christ, in the sight of God and our Father. 1 Thessalonians 1:3

Meditation Scriptures

Now our Lord Jesus Christ himself, and God, even our Father, which hath loved us, and hath given us everlasting consolation and good hope through grace. 2 Thessalonians 2:16

For the hope which is laid up for you in heaven, whereof ye heard before in the word of the truth of the gospel. Colossians 1:5

For what is our hope, or joy, or crown of rejoicing? Are not even ye in the presence of our Lord Jesus Christ at his coming?
1 Thessalonians 2:19

In hope of eternal life, which God, that cannot lie, promised before the world began. Titus 1:2

Looking for that blessed hope, and the glorious appearing of the great God and our Saviour Jesus Christ. Titus 2:13

That being justified by his grace, we should be made heirs according to the hope of eternal life. Titus 3:7

Meditation Scriptures

DELIVERANCE

He shall deliver thee in six troubles: yea, in seven there shall no evil touch thee. Job 5:19

But know that the Lord hath set apart him that is godly for himself: the Lord will hear when I call unto him. Psalm 4:3

The angel of the Lord encampeth round about them that fear him, and delivereth them. Psalm 34:7

Many are the afflictions of the righteous: but the Lord delivereth him out of them all. Psalm 34:19

For the Lord loveth judgment, and forsaketh not his saints; they are preserved for ever: but the seed of the wicked shall be cut off. Psalm 37:28

And lead us not into temptation, but deliver us from evil: For thine is the kingdom, and the power, and the glory, for ever. Amen. Matthew 6:13

He that believeth on him is not condemned: but he that believeth not is condemned already, because he hath not believed in the name of the only begotten Son of God. John 3:18

And ye shall know the truth, and the truth shall make you free. John 8:32

Knowing this, that our old man is crucified with him, that the body of sin might be destroyed, that henceforth we should not serve sin. Romans 6:6

For sin shall not have dominion over you: for ye are not under the law, but under grace. Romans 6:14

There hath no temptation taken you but such as is common to man: but God is faithful, who will not suffer you to be tempted above that ye are able; but will with the temptation also make a way to escape, that ye may be able to bear it. 1 Corinthians 10:13

Grace be to you and peace from God the Father, and from our Lord Jesus Christ, Who gave himself for our sins, that he might deliver us from this present evil world, according to the will of God and our Father. Galatians 1:3-4

But the Lord is faithful, who shall stablish you, and keep you from evil. 2 Thessalonians 3:3

For in that he himself hath suffered being tempted, he is able to succour them that are tempted. Hebrews 2:18

For the eyes of the Lord are over the righteous, and his ears are open unto their prayers: but the face of the Lord is against them that do evil. And who is he that will harm you, if ye be followers of that which is good? 1 Peter 3:12-13

The Lord knoweth how to deliver the godly out of temptations, and to reserve the unjust unto the day of judgment to be punished. 2 Peter 2:9

Meditation Scriptures

JOY

Then he said unto them, Go your way, eat the fat, and drink the sweet, and send portions unto them for whom nothing is prepared: for this day is holy unto our Lord: neither be ye sorry; for the joy of the Lord is your strength. Nehemiah 8:10

When the morning stars sang together, and all the sons of God shouted for joy? Job 38:7

Thou wilt shew me the path of life: in thy presence is fulness of joy; at thy right hand there are pleasures for evermore. Psalm 16:11

The king shall joy in thy strength, O Lord; and in thy salvation how greatly shall he rejoice! Psalm 21:1

For his anger endureth but a moment; in his favour is life: weeping may endure for a night, but joy cometh in the morning. Psalm 30:5

Let them shout for joy, and be glad, that favour my righteous cause: yea, let them say continually, Let the Lord be magnified, which hath pleasure in the prosperity of his servant. Psalm 35:27

Restore unto me the joy of thy salvation; and uphold me with thy free spirit. Psalm 51:12

They that sow in tears shall reap in joy. Psalm 126:5

Let the saints be joyful in glory: let them sing aloud upon their beds. Psalm 149:5

A man hath joy by the answer of his mouth: and a word spoken in due season, how good is it! Proverbs 15:23

It is joy to the just to do judgment: but destruction shall be to the workers of iniquity. Proverbs 21:15

Go thy way, eat thy bread with joy, and drink thy wine with a merry heart; for God now accepteth thy works. Ecclesiastes 9:7

And the ransomed of the Lord shall return, and come to Zion with songs and everlasting joy upon their heads: they shall obtain joy and gladness, and sorrow and sighing shall flee away. Isaiah 35:10

Therefore the redeemed of the Lord shall return, and come with singing unto Zion; and everlasting joy shall be upon their head: they shall obtain gladness and joy; and sorrow and mourning shall flee away. Isaiah 51:11

Break forth into joy, sing together, ye waste places of Jerusalem: for the Lord hath comforted his people, he hath redeemed Jerusalem. Isaiah 52:9

For ye shall go out with joy, and be led forth with peace: the mountains and the hills shall break forth before you into singing, and all the trees of the field shall clap their hands. Isaiah 55:12

And thou shalt have joy and gladness; and many shall rejoice at his birth. Luke 1:14

And the angel said unto them, Fear not: for, behold, I bring you good tidings of great joy, which shall be to all people. Luke 2:10

Rejoice ye in that day, and leap for joy: for, behold, your reward is great in heaven: for in the like manner did their fathers unto the prophets. Luke 6:23

Likewise, I say unto you, there is joy in the presence of the angels of God over one sinner that repenteth. Luke 15:10

And they worshipped him, and returned to Jerusalem with great joy. Luke 24:52

These things have I spoken unto you, that my joy might remain in you, and that your joy might be full. John 15:11

Verily, verily, I say unto you, That ye shall weep and lament, but the world shall rejoice: and ye shall be sorrowful, but your sorrow shall be turned into joy. John 16:20

A woman when she is in travail hath sorrow, because her hour is come: but as soon as she is delivered of the child, she remembereth no more the anguish, for joy that a man is born into the world. And ye now therefore have sorrow: but I will see you again, and your heart shall rejoice, and your joy no man taketh from you. And in that day ye shall ask me nothing. Verily, verily, I say unto you, Whatsoever ye shall ask the Father in my name, he will give it you. Hitherto have ye asked nothing in my name: ask, and ye shall receive, that your joy may be full. John 16:21-24

And now come I to thee; and these things I speak in the world, that they might have my joy fulfilled in themselves. John 17:13

Thou hast made known to me the ways of life; thou shalt make me full of joy with thy countenance. Acts 2:28

And the disciples were filled with joy, and with the Holy Ghost. Acts 13:52

And not only so, but we also joy in God through our Lord Jesus Christ, by whom we have now received the atonement. Romans 5:11

For the kingdom of God is not meat and drink; but righteousness, and peace, and joy in the Holy Ghost. Romans 14:17

Now the God of hope fill you with all joy and peace in believing, that ye may abound in hope, through the power of the Holy Ghost. Romans 15:13

That I may come unto you with joy by the will of God, and may with you be refreshed. Romans 15:32

Not for that we have dominion over your faith, but are helpers of your joy: for by faith ye stand. 2 Corinthians 1:24

Great is my boldness of speech toward you, great is my glorying of you: I am filled with comfort, I am exceeding joyful in all our tribulation. 2 Corinthians 7:4

And having this confidence, I know that I shall abide and continue with you all for your furtherance and joy of faith. Philippians 1:25

Strengthened with all might, according to his glorious power, unto all patience and longsuffering with joyfulness. Colossians 1:11

And ye became followers of us, and of the Lord, having received the word in much affliction, with joy of the Holy Ghost. 1 Thessalonians 1:6

For what is our hope, or joy, or crown of rejoicing? Are not even ye in the presence of our Lord Jesus Christ at his coming? For ye are our glory and joy. 1 Thessalonians 2:19-20

My brethren, count it all joy when ye fall into divers temptations. James 1:2

And these things write we unto you, that your joy may be full. 1 John 1:4

Now unto him that is able to keep you from falling, and to present you faultless before the presence of his glory with exceeding joy. Jude 1:24

Meditation Scriptures

PRAYER

Let us therefore come boldly unto the throne of grace, that we may obtain mercy, and find grace to help in time of need. Hebrews 4:16

If ye then, being evil, know how to give good gifts unto your children, how much more shall your Father which is in heaven give good things to them that ask him? Matthew 7:11

Ask, and it shall be given you; seek, and ye shall find; knock, and it shall be opened unto you: For every one that asketh receiveth; and he that seeketh findeth; and to him that knocketh it shall be opened. Or what man is there of you, whom if his son ask bread, will he give him a stone? Or if he ask a fish, will he give him a serpent? If ye then, being evil, know how to give good gifts unto your children, how much more shall your Father which is in heaven give good things to them that ask him? Matthew 7:7-11

Again I say unto you, That if two of you shall agree on earth as touching any thing that they shall ask, it shall be done for them of my Father which is in heaven. For where two or three are gathered together in my name, there am I in the midst of them. Matthew 18:19-20

And whatsoever ye shall ask in my name, that will I do, that the Father may be glorified in the Son. If ye shall ask any thing in my name, I will do it. John 14:13-14

But the Comforter, which is the Holy Ghost, whom the Father will send in my name, he shall teach you all things, and bring all things to your remembrance, whatsoever I have said unto you. John 14:26

Ye have not chosen me, but I have chosen you, and ordained you, that ye should go and bring forth fruit, and that your fruit should remain: that whatsoever ye shall ask of the Father in my name, he may give it you. John 15:16

And in that day ye shall ask me nothing. Verily, verily, I say unto you, Whatsoever ye shall ask the Father in my name, he will give it you. Hitherto have ye asked nothing in my name: ask, and ye shall receive, that your joy may be full. John 16:23-24

At that day ye shall ask in my name: and I say not unto you, that I will pray the Father for you. John 16:26

Is any sick among you? let him call for the elders of the church; and let them pray over him, anointing him with oil in the name of the Lord. James 5:14

After this manner therefore pray ye: Our Father which art in heaven, Hallowed be thy name. Thy kingdom come. Thy will be done in earth, as it is in heaven. Give us this day our daily bread. And forgive us our debts, as we forgive our debtors. And lead us not into temptation, but deliver us from evil: For thine is the kingdom, and the power, and the glory, for ever. Amen. Matthew 6:9-13

But know that the Lord hath set apart him that is godly for himself: the Lord will hear when I call unto him. Psalm 4:3

My voice shalt thou hear in the morning, O Lord; in the morning will I direct my prayer unto thee, and will look up. Psalm 5:3

I waited patiently for the Lord; and he inclined unto me, and heard my cry. Psalm 40:1

Evening, and morning, and at noon, will I pray, and cry aloud: and he shall hear my voice. Psalm 55:17

The Lord is far from the wicked: but he heareth the prayer of the righteous. Proverbs 15:29

The eyes of the Lord are upon the righteous, and his ears are open unto their cry. Psalm 34:15

Therefore I will look unto the Lord; I will wait for the God of my salvation: my God will hear me. Micah 7:7

And this is the confidence that we have in him, that, if we ask any thing according to his will, he heareth us: And if we know that he hear us, whatsoever we ask, we know that we have the petitions that we desired of him. 1 John 5:14-15

If I regard iniquity in my heart, the Lord will not hear me. Psalm 66:18

Whoso stoppeth his ears at the cry of the poor, he also shall cry himself, but shall not be heard. Proverbs 21:13

He that turneth away his ear from hearing the law, even his prayer shall be abomination. Proverbs 28:9

Behold, the Lord's hand is not shortened, that it cannot save; neither his ear heavy, that it cannot hear: But your iniquities have separated between you and your God, and your sins have hid his face from you, that he will not hear. Isaiah 59:1-2

Then shall they cry unto the Lord, but he will not hear them: he will even hide his face from them at that time, as they have behaved themselves ill in their doings. Micah 3:4

Ye lust, and have not: ye kill, and desire to have, and cannot obtain: ye fight and war, yet ye have not, because ye ask not. Ye ask, and receive not, because ye ask amiss, that ye may consume it upon your lusts. James 4:2-3

Likewise, ye husbands, dwell with them according to knowledge, giving honour unto the wife, as unto the weaker vessel, and as being heirs together of the grace of life; that your prayers be not hindered. 1 Peter 3:7

For the eyes of the Lord are over the righteous, and his ears are open unto their prayers: but the face of the Lord is against them that do evil. 1 Peter 3:12

And when thou prayest, thou shalt not be as the hypocrites are: for they love to pray standing in the synagogues and in the corners of the streets, that they may be seen of men. Verily I say unto you, They have their reward. But thou, when thou prayest, enter into thy closet, and when thou hast shut thy door, pray to thy Father which is in secret; and thy Father which seeth in secret shall reward thee openly. But when ye pray, use not vain repetitions, as the heathen do: for they think that they shall be heard for their much speaking. Be not ye therefore like unto them: for your Father knoweth what things ye have need of, before ye ask him. Matthew 6:5-8

For if ye forgive men their trespasses, your heavenly Father will also forgive you: But if ye forgive not men their trespasses, neither will your Father forgive your trespasses. Moreover when ye fast, be not, as the hypocrites, of a sad countenance: for they disfigure their faces, that they may appear unto men to fast. Verily I say unto you, They have their reward. But thou, when thou fastest, anoint thine head, and wash thy face; That thou appear not unto men to fast, but unto thy Father which is in secret: and thy Father, which seeth in secret, shall reward thee openly. Matthew 6:14-18

And when ye stand praying, forgive, if ye have ought against any: that your Father also which is in heaven may forgive you your trespasses. Mark 11:25

I cried to thee, O Lord; and unto the Lord I made supplication. Psalm 30:8

I will offer to thee the sacrifice of thanksgiving, and will call upon the name of the Lord. Psalm 116:17

And I set my face unto the Lord God, to seek by prayer and supplication, with fasting, and sackcloth, and ashes. Daniel 9:3

Praying always with all prayer and supplication in the Spirit, and watching thereunto with all perseverance and supplication for all saints. Ephesians 6:18

I exhort therefore, that, first of all, supplications, prayers, intercessions, and giving of thanks, be made for all men. 1 Timothy 2:1

How should one chase a thousand, and two put ten thousand to flight. Deuteronomy 32:30

This is the third time I am coming to you. In the mouth of two or three witnesses shall every word be established. 2 Corinthians 13:1

Verily I say unto you, Whatsoever ye shall bind on earth shall be bound in heaven: and whatsoever ye shall loose on earth shall be loosed in heaven. Again I say unto you, That if two of you shall agree on earth as touching any thing that they shall ask, it shall be done for them of my Father which is in heaven. Matthew 18:18-19

Jesus answered and said unto them, Verily I say unto you, If ye have faith, and doubt not, ye shall not only do this which is done to the fig tree, but also if ye shall say unto this mountain, Be thou removed, and be thou cast into the sea; it shall be done. And all things, whatsoever ye shall ask in prayer, believing, ye shall receive. Matthew 21:21-22

Jesus said unto him, If thou canst believe, all things are possible to him that believeth. And straightway the father of the child cried out, and said with tears, Lord, I believe; help thou mine unbelief. Mark 9:23-24

Therefore I say unto you, What things soever ye desire, when ye pray, believe that ye receive them, and ye shall have them. Mark 11:24

And the prayer of faith shall save the sick, and the Lord shall raise him up; and if he have committed sins, they shall be forgiven him. James 5:15

But they that wait upon the Lord shall renew their strength; they shall mount up with wings as eagles; they shall run, and not be weary; and they shall walk, and not faint. Isaiah 40:31

Call unto me, and I will answer thee, and shew thee great and mighty things, which thou knowest not. Jeremiah 33:3

Likewise the Spirit also helpeth our infirmities: for we know not what we should pray for as we ought: but the Spirit itself maketh intercession for us with groanings which cannot be uttered. And he that searcheth the hearts knoweth what is the mind of the Spirit, because he maketh intercession for the saints according to the will of God. Romans 8:26-27

For if I pray in an unknown tongue, my spirit prayeth, but my understanding is unfruitful. What is it then? I will pray with the spirit, and I will pray with the understanding also: I will sing with the spirit, and I will sing with the understanding also. 1 Corinthians 14:14-15

And for me, that utterance may be given unto me, that I may open my mouth boldly, to make known the mystery of the gospel, For which I am an ambassador in bonds: that therein I may speak boldly, as I ought to speak. Ephesians 6:19-20

But ye, beloved, building up yourselves on your most holy faith, praying in the Holy Ghost. Jude 1:20

And he saw that there was no man, and wondered that there was no intercessor: therefore his arm brought salvation unto him; and his right-eousness, it sustained him. Isaiah 59:16

And I sought for a man among them, that should make up the hedge, and stand in the gap before me for the land, that I should not destroy it: but I found none. Ezekiel 22:30

But I have prayed for thee, that thy faith fail not: and when thou art converted, strengthen thy brethren. Luke 22:32

At that day ye shall ask in my name: and I say not unto you, that I will pray the Father for you. John 16:26

I pray for them: I pray not for the world, but for them which thou hast given me; for they are thine. John 17:9

Neither pray I for these alone, but for them also which shall believe on me through their word. John 17:20

Brethren, my heart's desire and prayer to God for Israel is, that they might be saved. Romans 10:1

Now I beseech you, brethren, for the Lord Jesus Christ's sake, and for the love of the Spirit, that ye strive together with me in your prayers to God for me. Romans 15:30

For this cause we also, since the day we heard it, do not cease to pray for you, and to desire that ye might be filled with the knowledge of his will in all wisdom and spiritual understanding. Colossians 1:9

Withal praying also for us, that God would open unto us a door of utterance, to speak the mystery of Christ, for which I am also in bonds. Colossians 4:3

Wherefore also we pray always for you, that our God would count you worthy of this calling, and fulfil all the good pleasure of his goodness, and the work of faith with power. 2 Thessalonians 1:11

Finally, brethren, pray for us, that the word of the Lord may have free course, and be glorified, even as it is with you: And that we may be delivered from unreasonable and wicked men: for all men have not faith. 2 Thessalonians 3:1-2

Confess your faults one to another, and pray one for another, that ye may be healed. The effectual fervent prayer of a righteous man availeth much. James 5:16

And she was a widow of about fourscore and four years, which departed not from the temple, but served God with fastings and prayers night and day. Luke 2:37

Meditation Scriptures

FEAR

Fear not, little flock; for it is your Father's good pleasure to give you the kingdom. Luke 12:32

Peace I leave with you, my peace I give unto you: not as the world giveth, give I unto you. Let not your heart be troubled, neither let it be afraid. John 14:27

For ye have not received the spirit of bondage again to fear; but ye have received the Spirit of adoption, whereby we cry, Abba, Father. Romans 8:15

For God hath not given us the spirit of fear; but of power, and of love, and of a sound mind. 2 Timothy 1:7

There is no fear in love; but perfect love casteth out fear: because fear hath torment. He that feareth is not made perfect in love. 1 John 4:18

The fear of the wicked, it shall come upon him: but the desire of the righteous shall be granted. Proverbs 10:24

The fear of man bringeth a snare: but whoso putteth his trust in the Lord shall be safe. Proverbs 29:25

For the thing which I greatly feared is come upon me, and that which I was afraid of is come unto me. Job 3:25

And he answered, Fear not: for they that be with us are more than they that be with them. 2 Kings 6:16

For I the Lord thy God will hold thy right hand, saying unto thee, Fear not; I will help thee. Isaiah 41:13

Yea, though I walk through the valley of the shadow of death, I will fear no evil: for thou art with me; thy rod and thy staff they comfort me. Psalm 23:4

Meditation Scriptures

The Lord is my light and my salvation; whom shall I fear? the Lord is the strength of my life; of whom shall I be afraid? Psalm 27:1

Though an host should encamp against me, my heart shall not fear: though war should rise against me, in this will I be confident. Psalm 27:3

God is our refuge and strength, a very present help in trouble. Psalm 46:1

But whoso hearkeneth unto me shall dwell safely, and shall be quiet from fear of evil. Proverbs 1:33

When thou liest down, thou shalt not be afraid: yea, thou shalt lie down, and thy sleep shall be sweet. Be not afraid of sudden fear, neither of the desolation of the wicked, when it cometh. For the Lord shall be thy confidence, and shall keep thy foot from being taken. Proverbs 3:24-26

And it shall come to pass in the day that the Lord shall give thee rest from thy sorrow, and from thy fear, and from the hard bondage wherein thou wast made to serve. Isaiah 14:3

When thou passest through the waters, I will be with thee; and through the rivers, they shall not overflow thee: when thou walkest through the fire, thou shalt not be burned; neither shall the flame kindle upon thee. Isaiah 43:2

In God I will praise his word, in God I have put my trust; I will not fear what flesh can do unto me. Psalm 56:4

The Lord is on my side; I will not fear: what can man do unto me? Psalm 118:6

The fear of man bringeth a snare: but whoso putteth his trust in the Lord shall be safe. Proverbs 29:25

So that we may boldly say, The Lord is my helper, and I will not fear what man shall do unto me. Hebrews 13:6

And fear not them which kill the body, but are not able to kill the soul: but rather fear him which is able to destroy both soul and body in hell. Matthew 10:28

And who is he that will harm you, if ye be followers of that which is good? But and if ye suffer for righteousness' sake, happy are ye: and be not afraid of their terror, neither be troubled. 1 Peter 3:13-14

The fear of the Lord is clean, enduring for ever: the judgments of the Lord are true and righteous altogether. Psalm 19:9

The fear of the Lord is the beginning of wisdom: a good understanding have all they that do his commandments: his praise endureth for ever. Psalm 111:10

Then shalt thou understand the fear of the Lord, and find the knowledge of God. Proverbs 2:5

The fear of the Lord is the beginning of wisdom: and the knowledge of the holy is understanding. Proverbs 9:10

The fear of the Lord prolongeth days: but the years of the wicked shall be shortened. Proverbs 10:27

In the fear of the Lord is strong confidence: and his children shall have a place of refuge. The fear of the Lord is a fountain of life, to depart from the snares of death. Proverbs 14:26-27

The fear of the Lord is the instruction of wisdom; and before honour is humility. Proverbs 15:33

The fear of the Lord is to hate evil: pride, and arrogancy, and the evil way, and the froward mouth, do I hate. Proverbs 8:13

Better is little with the fear of the Lord than great treasure and trouble therewith. Proverbs 15:16

By mercy and truth iniquity is purged: and by the fear of the Lord men depart from evil. Proverbs 16:6

The fear of the Lord tendeth to life: and he that hath it shall abide satisfied; he shall not be visited with evil. Proverbs 19:23

By humility and the fear of the Lord are riches, and honour, and life. Proverbs 22:4

Having therefore these promises, dearly beloved, let us cleanse ourselves from all filthiness of the flesh and spirit, perfecting holiness in the fear of God. 2 Corinthians 7:1

Let not thine heart envy sinners: but be thou in the fear of the Lord all the day long. Proverbs 23:17

Meditation Scriptures

FAITH

But Jesus turned him about, and when he saw her, he said, Daughter, be of good comfort; thy faith hath made thee whole. And the woman was made whole from that hour. Matthew 9:22

Then Jesus answered and said unto her, O woman, great is thy faith: be it unto thee even as thou wilt. And her daughter was made whole from that very hour. Matthew 15:28

And he said unto her, Daughter, thy faith hath made thee whole; go in peace, and be whole of thy plague. Mark 5:34

When Jesus heard these things, he marvelled at him, and turned him about, and said unto the people that followed him, I say unto you, I have not found so great faith, no, not in Israel. Luke 7:9

And he said unto them, Where is your faith? And they being afraid wondered, saying one to another, What manner of man is this! for he commandeth even the winds and water, and they obey him. Luke 8:25

As it is written, I have made thee a father of many nations, before him whom he believed, even God, who quickeneth the dead, and calleth those things which be not as though they were. Who against hope believed in hope, that he might become the father of many nations; according to that which was spoken, So shall thy seed be. And being not weak in faith, he considered not his own body now dead, when he was about an hundred years old, neither yet the deadness of Sara's womb: He staggered not at the promise of God through unbelief; but was strong in faith, giving glory to God; And being fully persuaded that, what he had promised, he was able also to perform. Romans 4:17-21

Through faith also Sara herself received strength to conceive seed, and was delivered of a child when she was past age, because she judged him faithful who had promised. Therefore sprang there even of one, and him as good as dead, so many as the stars of the sky in multitude, and

as the sand which is by the sea shore innumerable. These all died in faith, not having received the promises, but having seen them afar off, and were persuaded of them, and embraced them, and confessed that they were strangers and pilgrims on the earth. Hebrews 11:11-13

For verily I say unto you, If ye have faith as a grain of mustard seed, ye shall say unto this mountain, Remove hence to yonder place; and it shall remove; and nothing shall be impossible unto you. Matthew 17:20

And Jesus answering saith unto them, Have faith in God. For verily I say unto you, That whosoever shall say unto this mountain, Be thou removed, and be thou cast into the sea; and shall not doubt in his heart, but shall believe that those things which he saith shall come to pass; he shall have whatsoever he saith. Therefore I say unto you, What things soever ye desire, when ye pray, believe that ye receive them, and ye shall have them. Mark 11:22-24

Then saith he to Thomas, reach hither thy finger, and behold my hands; and reach hither thy hand, and thrust it into my side: and be not faithless, but believing. John 20:27

Jesus saith unto him, Thomas, because thou hast seen me, thou hast believed: blessed are they that have not seen, and yet have believed. John 20:29

And he that doubteth is damned if he eat, because he eateth not of faith: for whatsoever is not of faith is sin. Romans 14:23

While we look not at the things which are seen, but at the things which are not seen: for the things which are seen are temporal; but the things which are not seen are eternal. 2 Corinthians 4:18

For we walk by faith, not by sight. 2 Corinthians 5:7

Let us hold fast the profession of our faith without wavering; for he is faithful that promised. Hebrews 10:23

Now faith is the substance of things hoped for, the evidence of things not seen. Hebrews 11:1

Through faith we understand that the worlds were framed by the word of God, so that things which are seen were not made of things which do appear. Hebrews 11:3

Knowing this, that the trying of your faith worketh patience. James 1:3

Whom having not seen, ye love; in whom, though now ye see him not, yet believing, ye rejoice with joy unspeakable and full of glory. Receiving the end of your faith, even the salvation of your souls. 1 Peter 1:8-9

But let him ask in faith, nothing wavering. For he that wavereth is like a wave of the sea driven with the wind and tossed. For let not that man think that he shall receive any thing of the Lord. A double minded man is unstable in all his ways. James 1:8

What doth it profit, my brethren, though a man say he hath faith, and have not works? can faith save him? If a brother or sister be naked, and destitute of daily food, And one of you say unto them, Depart in peace, be ye warmed and filled; notwithstanding ye give them not those things which are needful to the body; what doth it profit? Even so faith, if it hath not works, is dead, being alone. Yea, a man may say, Thou hast faith, and I have works: shew me thy faith without thy works, and I will shew thee my faith by my works. Thou believest that there is one God; thou doest well: the devils also believe, and tremble. But wilt thou know, O vain man, that faith without works is dead? Was not Abraham our father justified by works, when he had offered Isaac his son upon the altar? Seest thou how faith wrought with his works, and by works

was faith made perfect? And the scripture was fulfilled which saith, Abraham believed God, and it was imputed unto him for righteousness: and he was called the Friend of God. Ye see then how that by works a man is justified, and not by faith only. Likewise also was not Rahab the harlot justified by works, when she had received the messengers, and had sent them out another way? For as the body without the spirit is dead, so faith without works is dead also. James 2:14-26

Now in the morning as he returned into the city, he hungered. And when he saw a fig tree in the way, he came to it, and found nothing thereon, but leaves only, and said unto it, Let no fruit grow on thee henceforward for ever. And presently the fig tree withered away. And when the disciples saw it, they marvelled, saying, How soon is the fig tree withered away! Matthew 21:18-20

And seeing a fig tree afar off having leaves, he came, if haply he might find any thing thereon: and when he came to it, he found nothing but leaves; for the time of figs was not yet. And Jesus answered and said unto it, No man eat fruit of thee hereafter for ever. And his disciples heard it. Mark 11:13-14

And in the morning, as they passed by, they saw the fig tree dried up from the roots. And Peter calling to remembrance saith unto him, Master, behold, the fig tree which thou cursedst is withered away. Mark 11:20-21

Above all, taking the shield of faith, wherewith ye shall be able to quench all the fiery darts of the wicked. Ephesians 6:16

Fight the good fight of faith, lay hold on eternal life, whereunto thou art also called, and hast professed a good profession before many witnesses. 1 Timothy 6:12

But whoso hath this world's good, and seeth his brother have need, and shutteth up his bowels of compassion from him, how dwelleth the love of God in him? My little children, let us not love in word, neither in tongue; but in deed and in truth. 1 John 3:17-18

For therein is the righteousness of God revealed from faith to faith: as it is written, The just shall live by faith. Romans 1:17

But that no man is justified by the law in the sight of God, it is evident: for, The just shall live by faith. Galatians 3:11

Now the just shall live by faith: but if any man draw back, my soul shall have no pleasure in him. Hebrews 10:38

By whom also we have access by faith into this grace wherein we stand, and rejoice in hope of the glory of God. Romans 5:2

For by grace are ye saved through faith; and that not of yourselves: it is the gift of God. Ephesians 2:8

That the blessing of Abraham might come on the Gentiles through Jesus Christ; that we might receive the promise of the Spirit through faith. Galatians 3:14

Looking unto Jesus the author and finisher of our faith; who for the joy that was set before him endured the cross, despising the shame, and is set down at the right hand of the throne of God. Hebrews 12:2

So then faith cometh by hearing, and hearing by the word of God. Romans 10:17

For I say, through the grace given unto me, to every man that is among you, not to think of himself more highly than he ought to think; but to think soberly, according as God hath dealt to every man the measure of faith. Romans 12:3

We having the same spirit of faith, according as it is written, I believed, and therefore have I spoken; we also believe, and therefore speak. 2 Corinthians 4:13

Then touched he their eyes, saying, According to your faith be it unto you. Matthew 9:29

Then Jesus answered and said unto her, O woman, great is thy faith: be it unto thee even as thou wilt. And her daughter was made whole from that very hour. Matthew 15:28

And he said unto her, Daughter, thy faith hath made thee whole; go in peace, and be whole of thy plague. Mark 5:34

And Jesus said unto him, Go thy way; thy faith hath made thee whole. And immediately he received his sight, and followed Jesus in the way. Mark 10:52

Meditation Scriptures

MERCY

The Lord is longsuffering, and of great mercy, forgiving iniquity and transgression, and by no means clearing the guilty, visiting the iniquity of the fathers upon the children unto the third and fourth generation. Numbers 14:18

And shewing mercy unto thousands of them that love me and keep my commandments. Deuteronomy 5:10

Know therefore that the Lord thy God, he is God, the faithful God, which keepeth covenant and mercy with them that love him and keep his commandments to a thousand generations. Deuteronomy 7:9

And he said, Lord God of Israel, there is no God like thee, in heaven above, or on earth beneath, who keepest covenant and mercy with thy servants that walk before thee with all their heart. 1 Kings 8:23

O give thanks unto the Lord; for he is good; for his mercy endureth for ever. 1 Chronicles 16:34

And that he would shew thee the secrets of wisdom, that they are double to that which is! Know therefore that God exacteth of thee less than thine iniquity deserveth. Job 11:6

Surely goodness and mercy shall follow me all the days of my life: and I will dwell in the house of the Lord for ever. Psalm 23:6

All the paths of the Lord are mercy and truth unto such as keep his covenant and his testimonies. Psalm 25:10

I will be glad and rejoice in thy mercy: for thou hast considered my trouble; thou hast known my soul in adversities. Psalm 31:7

Many sorrows shall be to the wicked: but he that trusteth in the Lord, mercy shall compass him about. Psalm 32:10

Thy mercy, O Lord, is in the heavens; and thy faithfulness reacheth unto the clouds. Psalm 36:5

The wicked borroweth, and payeth not again: but the righteous sheweth mercy, and giveth. Psalm 37:21

But I am like a green olive tree in the house of God: I trust in the mercy of God for ever and ever. Psalm 52:8

Also unto thee, O Lord, belongeth mercy: for thou renderest to every man according to his work. Psalm 62:12

For thou, Lord, art good, and ready to forgive; and plenteous in mercy unto all them that call upon thee. Psalm 86:5

For great is thy mercy toward me: and thou hast delivered my soul from the lowest hell. Psalm 86:13

But thou, O Lord, art a God full of compassion, and gracious, longsuffering, and plenteous in mercy and truth. Psalm 86:15

Justice and judgment are the habitation of thy throne: mercy and truth shall go before thy face. Psalm 89:14

The Lord is merciful and gracious, slow to anger, and plenteous in mercy. Psalm 103:8

For as the heaven is high above the earth, so great is his mercy toward them that fear him. Psalm 103:11

Like as a father pitieth his children, so the Lord pitieth them that fear him. Psalm 103:13

But the mercy of the Lord is from everlasting to everlasting upon them that fear him, and his righteousness unto his children's children. Psalm 103:17

Help me, O Lord my God: O save me according to thy mercy. Psalm 109:26

The earth, O Lord, is full of thy mercy: teach me thy statutes. Psalm 119:64

The Lord is gracious, and full of compassion; slow to anger, and of great mercy. Psalm 145:8

Let not mercy and truth forsake thee: bind them about thy neck; write them upon the table of thine heart. Proverbs 3:3

He that despiseth his neighbour sinneth: but he that hath mercy on the poor, happy is he. Do they not err that devise evil? but mercy and truth shall be to them that devise good. Proverbs 14:21-22

He that followeth after righteousness and mercy findeth life, righteousness, and honour. Proverbs 21:21

He that covereth his sins shall not prosper: but whoso confesseth and forsaketh them shall have mercy. Proverbs 28:13

And therefore will the Lord wait, that he may be gracious unto you, and therefore will he be exalted, that he may have mercy upon you: for the Lord is a God of judgment: blessed are all they that wait for him. Isaiah 30:18

For my name's sake will I defer mine anger, and for my praise will I refrain for thee, that I cut thee not off. Isaiah 48:9

Let the wicked forsake his way, and the unrighteous man his thoughts: and let him return unto the Lord, and he will have mercy upon him; and to our God, for he will abundantly pardon. Isaiah 55:7

Blessed are the merciful: for they shall obtain mercy. Matthew 5:7

As concerning the gospel, they are enemies for your sakes: but as touching the election, they are beloved for the fathers' sakes. For the gifts and calling of God are without repentance. For as ye in times past have not believed God, yet have now obtained mercy through their unbelief: Even so have these also now not believed, that through your mercy they also may obtain mercy. For God hath concluded them all in unbelief, that he might have mercy upon all. Romans 11:28-32

But God, who is rich in mercy, for his great love wherewith he loved us. Ephesians 2:4

Not by works of righteousness which we have done, but according to his mercy he saved us, by the washing of regeneration, and renewing of the Holy Ghost. Titus 3:5

Let us therefore come boldly unto the throne of grace, that we may obtain mercy, and find grace to help in time of need. Hebrews 4:16

Behold, we count them happy which endure. Ye have heard of the patience of Job, and have seen the end of the Lord; that the Lord is very pitiful, and of tender mercy. James 5:11

Blessed be the God and Father of our Lord Jesus Christ, which according to his abundant mercy hath begotten us again unto a lively hope by the resurrection of Jesus Christ from the dead. 1 Peter 1:3

Which in time past were not a people, but are now the people of God: which had not obtained mercy, but now have obtained mercy. 1 Peter 2:10

Mercy unto you, and peace, and love, be multiplied. Jude 1:2

PERSEVERANCE

Know ye not that they which run in a race run all, but one receiveth the prize? So run, that ye may obtain. 1 Corinthians 9:24

The righteous also shall hold on his way, and he that hath clean hands shall be stronger and stronger. Job 17:9

I had fainted, unless I had believed to see the goodness of the Lord in the land of the living. Wait on the Lord: be of good courage, and he shall strengthen thine heart: wait, I say, on the Lord. Psalm 27:13-14

The Lord will perfect that which concerneth me: thy mercy, O Lord, endureth for ever: forsake not the works of thine own hands. Psalm 138:8

But the path of the just is as the shining light, that shineth more and more unto the perfect day. Proverbs 4:18

For a dream cometh through the multitude of business. Ecclesiastes 5:3

Whatsoever thy hand findeth to do, do it with thy might; for there is no work, nor device, nor knowledge, nor wisdom, in the grave, whither thou goest. Ecclesiastes 9:10

He giveth power to the faint; and to them that have no might he increaseth strength. Even the youths shall faint and be weary, and the young men shall utterly fall: But they that wait upon the Lord shall renew their strength; they shall mount up with wings as eagles; they shall run, and not be weary; and they shall walk, and not faint. Isaiah 40:29-31

Ask, and it shall be given you; seek, and ye shall find; knock, and it shall be opened unto you: Matthew 7:7

Wherefore seeing we also are compassed about with so great a cloud of witnesses, let us lay aside every weight, and the sin which doth so easily beset us, and let us run with patience the race that is set before us. Hebrews 12:1

Therefore, my beloved brethren, be ye stedfast, unmoveable, always abounding in the work of the Lord, forasmuch as ye know that your labour is not in vain in the Lord. 1 Corinthians 15:58

And let us not be weary in well doing: for in due season we shall reap, if we faint not. Galatians 6:9

I press toward the mark for the prize of the high calling of God in Christ Jesus. Philippians 3:14

Thou therefore endure hardness, as a good soldier of Jesus Christ. 2 Timothy 2:3

Now the just shall love by faith: but if any man draw back, my soul shall have no pleasure in him. Hebrews 10:38

And whatsoever ye do, do it heartily, as to the Lord, and not unto men. Colossians 3:23

And so, after he had patiently endured, he obtained the promise. Hebrews 6:15

I have fought a good fight, I have finished my course, I have kept the faith: Henceforth there is laid up for me a crown of righteousness, which the Lord, the righteous judge, shall give me at that day: and not to me only, but unto all them also that love his appearing. 2 Timothy 4:7-8

Let us hold fast the profession of our faith without wavering; for he is faithful that promised. Hebrews 10:23

Cast not away therefore your confidence, which hath great recompence of reward. For ye have need of patience, that, after ye have done the will of God, ye might receive the promise. Hebrews 10:35-36

Wherefore take unto you the whole armour of God, that ye may be able to withstand in the evil day, and having done all, to stand. Stand therefore, having your loins girt about with truth, and having on the breastplate of righteousness. Ephesians 6:13-14

Therefore, my brethren dearly beloved and longed for, my joy and crown, so stand fast in the Lord, my dearly beloved. Philippians 4:1

Rooted and built up in him, and stablished in the faith, as ye have been taught, abounding therein with thanksgiving. Colossians 2:7

Prove all things; hold fast that which is good. 1 Thessalonians 5:21

Watch ye, stand fast in the faith, quit you like men, be strong.
1 Corinthians 16:13

Of the Jews five times received I forty stripes save one. Thrice was I beaten with rods, once was I stoned, thrice I suffered shipwreck, a night and a day I have been in the deep; In journeyings often, in perils of waters, in perils of robbers, in perils by mine own countrymen, in perils by the heathen, in perils in the city, in perils in the wilderness, in perils in the sea, in perils among false brethren; In weariness and

painfulness, in watchings often, in hunger and thirst, in fastings often, in cold and nakedness. 2 Corinthians 11:24-27

We are troubled on every side, yet not distressed; we are perplexed, but not in despair; Persecuted, but not forsaken; cast down, but not destroyed. 2 Corinthians 4:8-9

For which cause we faint not; but though our outward man perish, yet the inward man is renewed day by day. For our light affliction, which is but for a moment, worketh for us a far more exceeding and eternal weight of glory. 2 Corinthians 4:16-17

And we desire that every one of you do shew the same diligence to the full assurance of hope unto the end. Hebrews 6:11

Meditation Scriptures

PATIENCE

Wait on the Lord: be of good courage, and he shall strengthen thine heart: wait, I say, on the Lord. Psalm 27:14

Rest in the Lord, and wait patiently for him: fret not thyself because of him who prospereth in his way, because of the man who bringeth wicked devices to pass. Cease from anger, and forsake wrath: fret not thyself in any wise to do evil. For evildoers shall be cut off: but those that wait upon the Lord, they shall inherit the earth. Psalm 37:7-9

Wait on the Lord, and keep his way, and he shall exalt thee to inherit the land: when the wicked are cut off, thou shalt see it. Psalm 37:34

I waited patiently for the Lord; and he inclined unto me, and heard my cry. Psalm 40:1

Better is the end of a thing than the beginning thereof: and the patient in spirit is better than the proud in spirit. Ecclesiastes 7:8

These wait all upon thee; that thou mayest give them their meat in due season. Psalm 104:27

Say not thou, I will recompense evil; but wait on the Lord, and he shall save thee. Proverbs 20:22

And it shall be said in that day, Lo, this is our God; we have waited for him, and he will save us: this is the Lord; we have waited for him, we will be glad and rejoice in his salvation. Isaiah 25:9

It is good that a man should both hope and quietly wait for the salvation of the Lord. Lamentations 3:26

In your patience possess ye your souls. Luke 21:19

To them who by patient continuance in well doing seek for glory and honour and immortality, eternal life. Romans 2:7

But if we hope for that we see not, then do we with patience wait for it. Romans 8:25

Strengthened with all might, according to his glorious power, unto all patience and longsuffering with joyfulness. Colossians 1:11

Now we exhort you, brethren, warn them that are unruly, comfort the feebleminded, support the weak, be patient toward all men.
1 Thessalonians 5:14

And the Lord direct your hearts into the love of God, and into the patient waiting for Christ. 2 Thessalonians 3:5

Wherefore seeing we also are compassed about with so great a cloud of witnesses, let us lay aside every weight, and the sin which doth so easily beset us, and let us run with patience the race that is set before us. Hebrews 12:1

Be patient therefore, brethren, unto the coming of the Lord. Behold, the husbandman waiteth for the precious fruit of the earth, and hath long patience for it, until he receive the early and latter rain. Be ye also patient; stablish your hearts: for the coming of the Lord draweth nigh. James 5:7-8

Take, my brethren, the prophets, who have spoken in the name of the Lord, for an example of suffering affliction, and of patience. James 5:10

Whereby are given unto us exceeding great and precious promises: that by these ye might be partakers of the divine nature, having escaped the corruption that is in the world through lust. 2 Peter 1:4

And to knowledge temperance; and to temperance patience; and to patience godliness. 2 Peter 1:6

The Lord is not slack concerning his promise, as some men count slackness; but is longsuffering to us-ward, not willing that any should perish, but that all should come to repentance. 2 Peter 3:9

Because thou hast kept the word of my patience, I also will keep thee from the hour of temptation, which shall come upon all the world, to try them that dwell upon the earth. Revelation 3:10

Here is the patience of the saints: here are they that keep the commandments of God, and the faith of Jesus. Revelation 14:12

And not only so, but we glory in tribulations also: knowing that tribulation worketh patience; And patience, experience; and experience, hope. And hope maketh not ashamed; because the love of God is shed abroad in our hearts by the Holy Ghost which is given unto us. Romans 5:3-5

Rejoicing in hope; patient in tribulation; continuing instant in prayer. Romans 12:12

Knowing this, that the trying of your faith worketh patience. But let patience have her perfect work, that ye may be perfect and entire, wanting nothing. James 1:3-4

But that on the good ground are they, which in an honest and good heart, having heard the word, keep it, and bring forth fruit with patience. Luke 8:15

For whatsoever things were written aforetime were written for our learning, that we through patience and comfort of the scriptures might have hope. Romans 15:4

And let us not be weary in well doing: for in due season we shall reap, if we faint not. Galatians 6:9

For all the promises of God in him are yea, and in him Amen, unto the glory of God by us. 2 Corinthians 1:20

That ye be not slothful, but followers of them who through faith and patience inherit the promises. Hebrews 6:12

And so, after he had patiently endured, he obtained the promise. Hebrews 6:15

For ye have need of patience, that, after ye have done the will of God, ye might receive the promise. For yet a little while, and he that shall come will come, and will not tarry. Now the just shall live by faith: but if any man draw back, my soul shall have no pleasure in him. But we are not of them who draw back unto perdition; but of them that believe to the saving of the soul. Hebrews 10:36-39

Who through faith subdued kingdoms, wrought righteousness, obtained promises, stopped the mouths of lions. Hebrews 11:33

Meditation Scriptures

Humility

Lord, thou hast heard the desire of the humble: thou wilt prepare their heart, thou wilt cause thine ear to hear. Psalm 10:17

The humble shall see this, and be glad: and your heart shall live that seek God. Psalm 69:32

Lord, my heart is not haughty, nor mine eyes lofty: neither do I exercise myself in great matters, or in things too high for me. Surely I have behaved and quieted myself, as a child that is weaned of his mother: my soul is even as a weaned child. Psalm 131:1-2

Though the Lord be high, yet hath he respect unto the lowly: but the proud he knoweth afar off. Psalm 138:6

The Lord lifteth up the meek: he casteth the wicked down to the ground. Psalm 147:6

For the Lord taketh pleasure in his people: he will beautify the meek with salvation. Psalm 149:4

The fear of the Lord is the instruction of wisdom; and before honour is humility. Proverbs 15:33

For all those things hath mine hand made, and those things have been, saith the Lord: but to this man will I look, even to him that is poor and of a contrite spirit, and trembleth at my word. Isaiah 66:2

He hath shewed thee, O man, what is good; and what doth the Lord require of thee, but to do justly, and to love mercy, and to walk humbly with thy God? Micah 6:8

Blessed are the poor in spirit: for theirs is the kingdom of heaven. Matthew 5:3

But it shall not be so among you: but whosoever will be great among you, let him be your minister; And whosoever will be chief among you, let him be your servant. Matthew 20:26-27

And whosoever shall exalt himself shall be abased; and he that shall humble himself shall be exalted. Matthew 23:12

He hath put down the mighty from their seats, and exalted them of low degree. Luke 1:52

But when thou art bidden, go and sit down in the lowest room; that when he that bade thee cometh, he may say unto thee, Friend, go up higher: then shalt thou have worship in the presence of them that sit at meat with thee. Luke 14:10

And the publican, standing afar off, would not lift up so much as his eyes unto heaven, but smote upon his breast, saying, God be merciful to me a sinner. I tell you, this man went down to his house justified rather than the other: for every one that exalteth himself shall be abased; and he that humbleth himself shall be exalted. Luke 18:13-14

And there was also a strife among them, which of them should be accounted the greatest. And he said unto them, The kings of the Gentiles exercise lordship over them; and they that exercise authority upon them are called benefactors. But ye shall not be so: but he that is greatest among you, let him be as the younger; and he that is chief, as he that doth serve. For whether is greater, he that sitteth at meat, or he that serveth? is not he that sitteth at meat? but I am among you as he that serveth. Luke 22:24-27

He must increase, but I must decrease. John 3:30

Be of the same mind one toward another. Mind not high things, but condescend to men of low estate. Be not wise in your own conceits. Romans 12:16

But by the grace of God I am what I am: and his grace which was bestowed upon me was not in vain; but I laboured more abundantly than they all: yet not I, but the grace of God which was with me. 1 Corinthians 15:10

With all lowliness and meekness, with longsuffering, forbearing one another in love. Ephesians 4:2

I know both how to be abased, and I know how to abound: every where and in all things I am instructed both to be full and to be hungry, both to abound and to suffer need. Philippians 4:12

Let the brother of low degree rejoice in that he is exalted: But the rich, in that he is made low: because as the flower of the grass he shall pass away. James 1:9-10

Humble yourselves in the sight of the Lord, and he shall lift you up. James 4:10

Likewise, ye younger, submit yourselves unto the elder. Yea, all of you be subject one to another, and be clothed with humility: for God resisteth the proud, and giveth grace to the humble. Humble yourselves therefore under the mighty hand of God, that he may exalt you in due time. 1 Peter 5:5-6

Take my yoke upon you, and learn of me; for I am meek and lowly in heart: and ye shall find rest unto your souls. Matthew 11:29

If I then, your Lord and Master, have washed your feet; ye also ought to wash one another's feet. For I have given you an example, that ye should do as I have done to you. Verily, verily, I say unto you, The servant is not greater than his lord; neither he that is sent greater than he that sent him. John 13:14-16

Let nothing be done through strife or vainglory; but in lowliness of mind let each esteem other better than themselves. Look not every man on his own things, but every man also on the things of others. Let this mind be in you, which was also in Christ Jesus: Who, being in the form of God, thought it not robbery to be equal with God: But made himself of no reputation, and took upon him the form of a servant, and was made in the likeness of men: And being found in fashion as a man, he humbled himself, and became obedient unto death, even the death of the cross. Wherefore God also hath highly exalted him, and given him a name which is above every name: That at the name of Jesus every knee should bow, of things in heaven, and things in earth, and things under the earth; And that every tongue should confess that Jesus Christ is Lord, to the glory of God the Father. Philippians 2:3-11

Meditation Scriptures

MEEKNESS

Now the man Moses was very meek, above all the men which were upon the face of the earth. Numbers 12:3

The meek shall eat and be satisfied: they shall praise the Lord that seek him: your heart shall live for ever. Psalm 22:26

The meek will he guide in judgment: and the meek will he teach his way. Psalm 25:9

But the meek shall inherit the earth; and shall delight themselves in the abundance of peace. Psalm 37:11

And in thy majesty ride prosperously because of truth and meekness and righteousness; and thy right hand shall teach thee terrible things. Psalm 45:4

When God arose to judgment, to save all the meek of the earth. Selah. Psalm 76:9

The Lord lifteth up the meek: he casteth the wicked down to the ground. Psalm 147:6

For the Lord taketh pleasure in his people: he will beautify the meek with salvation. Psalm 149:4

But with righteousness shall he judge the poor, and reprove with equity for the meek of the earth: and he shall smite the earth with the rod of his mouth, and with the breath of his lips shall he slay the wicked. Isaiah 11:4

The meek also shall increase their joy in the Lord, and the poor among men shall rejoice in the Holy One of Israel. Isaiah 29:19

The Spirit of the Lord God is upon me; because the Lord hath anointed me to preach good tidings unto the meek; he hath sent me to bind up the brokenhearted, to proclaim liberty to the captives, and the opening of the prison to them that are bound. Isaiah 61:1

Seek ye the Lord, all ye meek of the earth, which have wrought his judgment; seek righteousness, seek meekness: it may be ye shall be hid in the day of the Lord's anger. Zephaniah 2:3

Blessed are the meek: for they shall inherit the earth. Matthew 5:5

Take my yoke upon you, and learn of me; for I am meek and lowly in heart: and ye shall find rest unto your souls. Matthew 11:29

Tell ye the daughter of Sion, Behold, thy King cometh unto thee, meek, and sitting upon an ass, and a colt the foal of an ass. Matthew 21:5

What will ye? shall I come unto you with a rod, or in love, and in the spirit of meekness? 1 Corinthians 4:21

Now I Paul myself beseech you by the meekness and gentleness of Christ, who in presence am base among you, but being absent am bold toward you. 2 Corinthians 10:1

But the fruit of the Spirit is love, joy, peace, longsuffering, gentleness, goodness, faith, Meekness, temperance: against such there is no law. Galatians 5:22-23

Brethren, if a man be overtaken in a fault, ye which are spiritual, restore such an one in the spirit of meekness; considering thyself, lest thou also be tempted. Galatians 6:1

Morning Glory

With all lowliness and meekness, with longsuffering, forbearing one another in love. Ephesians 4:2

Put on therefore, as the elect of God, holy and beloved, bowels of mercies, kindness, humbleness of mind, meekness, longsuffering. Colossians 3:12

But thou, O man of God, flee these things; and follow after righteousness, godliness, faith, love, patience, meekness. 1 Timothy 6:11

To speak evil of no man, to be no brawlers, but gentle, shewing all meekness unto all men. Titus 3:2

Wherefore lay apart all filthiness and superfluity of naughtiness, and receive with meekness the engrafted word, which is able to save your souls. James 1:21

Who is a wise man and endued with knowledge among you? let him shew out of a good conversation his works with meekness of wisdom. James 3:13

But let it be the hidden man of the heart, in that which is not corruptible, even the ornament of a meek and quiet spirit, which is in the sight of God of great price. 1 Peter 3:4

But sanctify the Lord God in your hearts: and be ready always to give an answer to every man that asketh you a reason of the hope that is in you with meekness and fear. 1 Peter 3:15

Meditation Scriptures

Meditation Scriptures

UNDERSTANDING

Discretion shall preserve thee, understanding shall keep thee. Proverbs 2:11

Good understanding giveth favour: but the way of transgressors is hard. Proverbs 13:15

Understanding is a wellspring of life unto him that hath it: but the instruction of fools is folly. Proverbs 16:22

Through wisdom is an house builded; and by understanding it is established. Proverbs 24:3

With thy wisdom and with thine understanding thou hast gotten thee riches, and hast gotten gold and silver into thy treasures. Ezekiel 28:4

But there is a spirit in man: and the inspiration of the Almighty giveth them understanding. Job 32:8

Who hath put wisdom in the inward parts? or who hath given understanding to the heart? Job 38:36

For the Lord giveth wisdom: out of his mouth cometh knowledge and understanding. Proverbs 2:6

The fear of the Lord is the beginning of wisdom: and the knowledge of the holy is understanding. Proverbs 9:10

There is no wisdom nor understanding nor counsel against the Lord. Proverbs 21:30

Then opened he their understanding, that they might understand the scriptures. Luke 24:25

The eyes of your understanding being enlightened; that ye may know what is the hope of his calling, and what the riches of the glory of his inheritance in the saints. Ephesians 1:18

Consider what I say; and the Lord give thee understanding in all things. 2 Timothy 2:7

And we know that the Son of God is come, and hath given us an understanding, that we may know him that is true, and we are in him that is true, even in his Son Jesus Christ. This is the true God, and eternal life. 1 John 5:20

The fear of the Lord is the beginning of wisdom: a good understanding have all they that do his commandments: his praise endureth for ever. Psalm 111:10

Through thy precepts I get understanding: therefore I hate every false way. Psalm 119:104

The entrance of thy words giveth light; it giveth understanding unto the simple. Psalm 119:130

So that thou incline thine ear unto wisdom, and apply thine heart to understanding. Proverbs 2:2

Let not mercy and truth forsake thee: bind them about thy neck; write them upon the table of thine heart: So shalt thou find favour and good understanding in the sight of God and man. Trust in the Lord with all thine heart; and lean not unto thine own understanding. Proverbs 3:3-5

And to love him with all the heart, and with all the understanding, and with all the soul, and with all the strength, and to love his neighbour as himself, is more than all whole burnt offerings and sacrifices. Mark 12:33

Hear, ye children, the instruction of a father, and attend to know understanding. Proverbs 4:1

Get wisdom, get understanding: forget it not; neither decline from the words of my mouth. Proverbs 4:5

Happy is the man that findeth wisdom, and the man that getteth understanding. Proverbs 3:13

Wisdom is the principal thing; therefore get wisdom: and with all thy getting get understanding. Proverbs 4:7

My son, attend unto my wisdom, and bow thine ear to my understanding. Proverbs 5:1

Doth not wisdom cry? and understanding put forth her voice? Proverbs 8:1

Counsel is mine, and sound wisdom: I am understanding; I have strength. Proverbs 8:14

How much better is it to get wisdom than gold! and to get understanding rather to be chosen than silver! Proverbs 16:16

He that getteth wisdom loveth his own soul: he that keepeth understanding shall find good. Proverbs 19:8

Wherefore be ye not unwise, but understanding what the will of the Lord is. Ephesians 5:17

For this cause we also, since the day we heard it, do not cease to pray for you, and to desire that ye might be filled with the knowledge of his will in all wisdom and spiritual understanding. Colossians 1:9

And unto man he said, Behold, the fear of the Lord, that is wisdom; and to depart from evil is understanding. Job 28:28

My mouth shall speak of wisdom; and the meditation of my heart shall be of understanding. Psalm 49:3

Give me understanding, and I shall keep thy law; yea, I shall observe it with my whole heart. Psalm 119:34

I have more understanding than all my teachers: for thy testimonies are my meditation. Psalm 119:99

A wise man will hear, and will increase learning; and a man of understanding shall attain unto wise counsels. Proverbs 1:5

Wisdom resteth in the heart of him that hath understanding: but that which is in the midst of fools is made known. Proverbs 14:33

The heart of him that hath understanding seeketh knowledge: but the mouth of fools feedeth on foolishness. Proverbs 15:14

Wisdom is before him that hath understanding; but the eyes of a fool are in the ends of the earth. Proverbs 17:24

He that hath knowledge spareth his words: and a man of understanding is of an excellent spirit. Even a fool, when he holdeth his peace, is counted wise: and he that shutteth his lips is esteemed a man of understanding. Proverbs 17:27-28

And I have filled him with the spirit of God, in wisdom, and in understanding, and in knowledge, and in all manner of workmanship. Exodus 31:3

And God gave Solomon wisdom and understanding exceeding much, and largeness of heart, even as the sand that is on the sea shore. 1 Kings 4:29

He was a widow's son of the tribe of Naphtali, and his father was a man of Tyre, a worker in brass: and he was filled with wisdom, and understanding, and cunning to work all works in brass. And he came to king Solomon, and wrought all his work. 1 Kings 7:14

And the spirit of the Lord shall rest upon him, the spirit of wisdom and understanding, the spirit of counsel and might, the spirit of knowledge and of the fear of the Lord. Isaiah 11:2

And I will give you pastors according to mine heart, which shall feed you with knowledge and understanding. Jeremiah 3:15

Children in whom was no blemish, but well favoured, and skilful in all wisdom, and cunning in knowledge, and understanding science, and such as had ability in them to stand in the king's palace, and whom they might teach the learning and the tongue of the Chaldeans. Daniel 1:4

As for these four children, God gave them knowledge and skill in all learning and wisdom: and Daniel had understanding in all visions and dreams. Daniel 1:17

And in all matters of wisdom and understanding, that the king inquired of them, he found them ten times better than all the magicians and astrologers that were in all his realm. Daniel 1:20

And he changeth the times and the seasons: he removeth kings, and setteth up kings: he giveth wisdom unto the wise, and knowledge to them that know understanding. Daniel 2:21

Meditation Scriptures

THE VOICE OF GOD

Yea, a sword shall pierce through thy own soul also, that the thoughts of many hearts may be revealed. Luke 2:35

And take the helmet of salvation, and the sword of the Spirit, which is the word of God. Ephesians 6:17

For the word of God is quick, and powerful, and sharper than any twoedged sword, piercing even to the dividing asunder of soul and spirit, and of the joints and marrow, and is a discerner of the thoughts and intents of the heart. Hebrews 4:12

And then shall that Wicked be revealed, whom the Lord shall consume with the spirit of his mouth, and shall destroy with the brightness of his coming. 2 Thessalonians 2:8

And he had in his right hand seven stars: and out of his mouth went a sharp twoedged sword: and his countenance was as the sun shineth in his strength. Revelation 1:16

And to the angel of the church in Pergamos write; These things saith he which hath the sharp sword with two edges. Revelation 2:12

Repent; or else I will come unto thee quickly, and will fight against them with the sword of my mouth. Revelation 2:16

And out of his mouth goeth a sharp sword, that with it he should smite the nations: and he shall rule them with a rod of iron: and he treadeth the winepress of the fierceness and wrath of Almighty God. Revelation 19:15

So then faith cometh by hearing, and hearing by the word of God. Romans 10:17

For whosoever shall call upon the name of the Lord shall be saved. How then shall they call on him in whom they have not believed? and how shall they believe in him of whom they have not heard? and how shall they hear without a preacher? Romans 10:13-14

Now when they heard this, they were pricked in their heart, and said unto Peter and to the rest of the apostles, Men and brethren, what shall we do? Acts 2:37

When they heard that, they were cut to the heart, and took counsel to slay them. Acts 5:33

When they heard these things, they were cut to the heart, and they gnashed on him with their teeth. Acts 7:54

When the even was come, they brought unto him many that were possessed with devils: and he cast out the spirits with his word, and healed all that were sick: Matthew 8:16

And when the tempter came to him, he said, If thou be the Son of God, command that these stones be made bread. But he answered and said, It is written, Man shall not live by bread alone, but by every word that proceedeth out of the mouth of God. Then the devil taketh him up into the holy city, and setteth him on a pinnacle of the temple, And saith unto him, If thou be the Son of God, cast thyself down: for it is written, He shall give his angels charge concerning thee: and in their hands they shall bear thee up, lest at any time thou dash thy foot against a stone. Jesus said unto him, It is written again, Thou shalt not tempt the Lord thy God. Again, the devil taketh him up into an exceeding high mountain, and sheweth him all the kingdoms of the world, and the glory of them; And saith unto him, All these things will I give thee, if thou wilt fall down and worship me. Then saith Jesus unto him, Get thee hence, Satan: for it is written, Thou shalt worship the Lord thy God, and him only shalt thou serve. Then the devil leaveth him, and, behold, angels came and ministered unto him. Matthew 4:3-11

MEDITATING ON GOD'S WORD

This book of the law shall not depart out of thy mouth; but thou shalt meditate therein day and night, that thou mayest observe to do according to all that is written therein: for then thou shalt make thy way prosperous, and then thou shalt have good success. Joshua 1:8

But his delight is in the law of the Lord; and in his law doth he meditate day and night. Psalm 1:2

Give ear to my words, O Lord, consider my meditation. Psalm 5:1

Let the words of my mouth, and the meditation of my heart, be acceptable in thy sight, O Lord, my strength, and my redeemer. Psalm 19:14

My mouth shall speak of wisdom; and the meditation of my heart shall be of understanding. Psalm 49:3

When I remember thee upon my bed, and meditate on thee in the night watches. Psalm 63:6

I will meditate also of all thy work, and talk of thy doings. Psalm 77:12

My meditation of him shall be sweet: I will be glad in the Lord. Psalm 104:34

I will meditate in thy precepts, and have respect unto thy ways. Psalm 119:15

Princes also did sit and speak against me: but thy servant did meditate in thy statutes. Psalm 119:23

My hands also will I lift up unto thy commandments, which I have loved; and I will meditate in thy statutes. Psalm 119:48

Let the proud be ashamed; for they dealt perversely with me without a cause: but I will meditate in thy precepts. Psalm 119:78

O how love I thy law! it is my meditation all the day. Psalm 119:97

I have more understanding than all my teachers: for thy testimonies are my meditation. Psalm 119:99

Mine eyes prevent the night watches, that I might meditate in thy word. Psalm 119:148

I remember the days of old; I meditate on all thy works; I muse on the work of thy hands. Psalm 143:5

Till I come, give attendance to reading, to exhortation, to doctrine. Meditate upon these things; give thyself wholly to them; that thy profiting may appear to all. 1 Timothy 4:13,15

Meditation Scriptures

HEALING

But he was wounded for our transgressions, he was bruised for our iniquities: the chastisement of our peace was upon him; and with his stripes we are healed. Isaiah 53:5

Who his own self bare our sins in his own body on the tree, that we, being dead to sins, should live unto righteousness: by whose stripes ye were healed. 1 Peter 2:24

And said, If thou wilt diligently hearken to the voice of the Lord thy God, and wilt do that which is right in his sight, and wilt give ear to his commandments, and keep all his statutes, I will put none of these diseases upon thee, which I have brought upon the Egyptians: for I am the Lord that healeth thee. Exodus 15:26

Thou shalt therefore keep the commandments, and the statutes, and the judgments, which I command thee this day, to do them. Wherefore it shall come to pass, if ye hearken to these judgments, and keep, and do them, that the Lord thy God shall keep unto thee the covenant and the mercy which he sware unto thy fathers: And he will love thee, and bless thee, and multiply thee: he will also bless the fruit of thy womb, and the fruit of thy land, thy corn, and thy wine, and thine oil, the increase of thy kine, and the flocks of thy sheep, in the land which he sware unto thy fathers to give thee. Thou shalt be blessed above all people: there shall not be male or female barren among you, or among your cattle. And the Lord will take away from thee all sickness, and will put none of the evil diseases of Egypt, which thou knowest, upon thee; but will lay them upon all them that hate thee. Deuteronomy 7:11-15

Trust in the Lord with all thine heart; and lean not unto thine own understanding. In all thy ways acknowledge him, and he shall direct thy paths. Be not wise in thine own eyes: fear the Lord, and depart from evil. It shall be health to thy navel, and marrow to thy bones. Proverbs 3:5-8

And ye shall serve the Lord your God, and he shall bless thy bread, and thy water; and I will take sickness away from the midst of thee. Exodus 23:25

Behold, thou hast instructed many, and thou hast strengthened the weak hands. Thy words have upholden him that was falling, and thou hast strengthened the feeble knees. Job 4:3-4

O Lord my God, I cried unto thee, and thou hast healed me. Psalm 30:2

He keepeth all his bones: not one of them is broken. Psalm 34:20

The Lord will strengthen him upon the bed of languishing: thou wilt make all his bed in his sickness. Psalm 41:3

Why art thou cast down, O my soul? and why art thou disquieted within me? hope thou in God: for I shall yet praise him, who is the health of my countenance, and my God. Psalm 42:11

Surely he shall deliver thee from the snare of the fowler, and from the noisome pestilence. Psalm 91:3

There shall no evil befall thee, neither shall any plague come nigh thy dwelling. Psalm 91:10

Who forgiveth all thine iniquities; who healeth all thy diseases. Who redeemeth thy life from destruction; who crowneth thee with lovingkindness and tender mercies; Who satisfieth thy mouth with good things; so that thy youth is renewed like the eagle's. Psalm 103:3-5

He sent his word, and healed them, and delivered them from their destructions. Psalm 107:20

The Lord upholdeth all that fall, and raiseth up all those that be bowed down. Psalm 145:14

The Lord openeth the eyes of the blind: the Lord raiseth them that are bowed down: the Lord loveth the righteous. Psalm 146:8

He healeth the broken in heart, and bindeth up their wounds. Psalm 147:3

My son, attend to my words; incline thine ear unto my sayings. Let them not depart from thine eyes; keep them in the midst of thine heart. For they are life unto those that find them, and health to all their flesh. Proverbs 4:20-22

For by me thy days shall be multiplied, and the years of thy life shall be increased. Proverbs 9:11

A sound heart is the life of the flesh: but envy the rottenness of the bones. Proverbs 14:30

Pleasant words are as an honeycomb, sweet to the soul, and health to the bones. Proverbs 16:24

Strengthen ye the weak hands, and confirm the feeble knees. Isaiah 35:3

He giveth power to the faint; and to them that have no might he increaseth strength. Isaiah 40:29

And the Lord shall guide thee continually, and satisfy thy soul in drought, and make fat thy bones: and thou shalt be like a watered garden, and like a spring of water, whose waters fail not. Isaiah 58:11

And when ye see this, your heart shall rejoice, and your bones shall flourish like an herb: and the hand of the Lord shall be known toward his servants, and his indignation toward his enemies. Isaiah 66:14

Heal me, O Lord, and I shall be healed; save me, and I shall be saved: for thou art my praise. Jeremiah 17:14

For I will restore health unto thee, and I will heal thee of thy wounds, saith the Lord; because they called thee an Outcast, saying, This is Zion, whom no man seeketh after. Jeremiah 30:17

Behold, I will bring it health and cure, and I will cure them, and will reveal unto them the abundance of peace and truth. Jeremiah 33:6

For I will cleanse their blood that I have not cleansed: for the Lord dwelleth in Zion. Joel 3:21

And they that were vexed with unclean spirits: and they were healed. And the whole multitude sought to touch him: for there went virtue out of him, and healed them all. Luke 6:18-19

Christ hath redeemed us from the curse of the law, being made a curse for us: for it is written, Cursed is every one that hangeth on a tree. Galatians 3:13

Wherefore lift up the hands which hang down, and the feeble knees; And make straight paths for your feet, lest that which is lame be turned out of the way; but let it rather be healed. Hebrews 12:12-13

Beloved, I wish above all things that thou mayest prosper and be in health, even as thy soul prospereth. 3 John 1:2

So Abraham prayed unto God: and God healed Abimelech, and his wife, and his maidservants; and they bare children. Genesis 20:17

There shall nothing cast their young, nor be barren, in thy land: the number of thy days I will fulfil. Exodus 23:26

He maketh the barren woman to keep house, and to be a joyful mother of children. Praise ye the Lord. Psalm 113:9

Lo, children are an heritage of the Lord: and the fruit of the womb is his reward. As arrows are in the hand of a mighty man; so are children of the youth. Happy is the man that hath his quiver full of them: they shall not be ashamed, but they shall speak with the enemies in the gate. Psalm 127:3-5

Thy wife shall be as a fruitful vine by the sides of thine house: thy children like olive plants round about thy table. Psalm 128:3

The Lord shall increase you more and more, you and your children. Psalm 115:14

Is any among you afflicted? let him pray. Is any merry? let him sing Psalms. Is any sick among you? let him call for the elders of the church; and let them pray over him, anointing him with oil in the name of the Lord: And the prayer of faith shall save the sick, and the Lord shall raise him up; and if he have committed sins, they shall be forgiven him. Confess your faults one to another, and pray one for another, that ye may be healed. The effectual fervent prayer of a righteous man availeth much. James 5:13-16

Meditation Scriptures

Meditation Scriptures

IN HIM

But to us there is but one God, the Father, of whom are all things, and we in him; and one Lord Jesus Christ, by whom are all things, and we by him. 1 Corinthians 8:6

For all the promises of God in him are yea, and in him Amen, unto the glory of God by us. 2 Corinthians 1:20

For he hath made him to be sin for us, who knew no sin; that we might be made the righteousness of God in him. 2 Corinthians 5:21

For though he was crucified through weakness, yet he liveth by the power of God. For we also are weak in him, but we shall live with him by the power of God toward you. 2 Corinthians 13:4

According as he hath chosen us in him before the foundation of the world, that we should be holy and without blame before him in love. Ephesians 1:4

That in the dispensation of the fulness of times he might gather together in one all things in Christ, both which are in heaven, and which are on earth; even in him. Ephesians 1:10

And be found in him, not having mine own righteousness, which is of the law, but that which is through the faith of Christ, the righteousness which is of God by faith. Philippians 3:9

For it pleased the Father that in him should all fulness dwell. Colossians 1:19

For in him dwelleth all the fulness of the Godhead bodily. And ye are complete in him, which is the head of all principality and power. Colossians 2:9-10

That the name of our Lord Jesus Christ may be glorified in you, and ye in him, according to the grace of our God and the Lord Jesus Christ. 2 Thessalonians 1:12

And again, I will put my trust in him. And again, Behold I and the children which God hath given me. Hebrews 2:13

Now the just shall live by faith: but if any man draw back, my soul shall have no pleasure in him. Hebrews 10:38

This then is the message which we have heard of him, and declare unto you, that God is light, and in him is no darkness at all. 1 John 1:5

But the anointing which ye have received of him abideth in you, and ye need not that any man teach you: but as the same anointing teacheth you of all things, and is truth, and is no lie, and even as it hath taught you, ye shall abide in him. And now, little children, abide in him; that, when he shall appear, we may have confidence, and not be ashamed before him at his coming. 1 John 2:27-28

And every man that hath this hope in him purifieth himself, even as he is pure. 1 John 3:3

And ye know that he was manifested to take away our sins; and in him is no sin. Whosoever abideth in him sinneth not: whosoever sinneth hath not seen him, neither known him. 1 John 3:5-6

Hereby know we that we dwell in him, and he in us, because he hath given us of his Spirit. 1 John 4:13

And this is the confidence that we have in him, that, if we ask any thing according to his will, he heareth us. 1 John 5:14

And we know that the Son of God is come, and hath given us an understanding, that we may know him that is true, and we are in him that is true, even in his Son Jesus Christ. This is the true God, and eternal life. 1 John 5:20

Meditation Scriptures

FORGIVENESS

For if ye turn again unto the Lord, your brethren and your children shall find compassion before them that lead them captive, so that they shall come again into this land: for the Lord your God is gracious and merciful, and will not turn away his face from you, if ye return unto him. 2 Chronicles 30:9

Blessed is he whose transgression is forgiven, whose sin is covered. Blessed is the man unto whom the Lord imputeth not iniquity, and in whose spirit there is no guile. Psalm 32:1-2

I acknowledged my sin unto thee, and mine iniquity have I not hid. I said, I will confess my transgressions unto the Lord; and thou forgavest the iniquity of my sin. Selah. Psalm 32:5

And the inhabitant shall not say, I am sick: the people that dwell therein shall be forgiven their iniquity. Isaiah 33:24

I have blotted out, as a thick cloud, thy transgressions, and, as a cloud, thy sins: return unto me; for I have redeemed thee. Isaiah 44:22

Who is a God like unto thee, that pardoneth iniquity, and passeth by the transgression of the remnant of his heritage? he retaineth not his anger for ever, because he delighteth in mercy. He will turn again, he will have compassion upon us; he will subdue our iniquities; and thou wilt cast all their sins into the depths of the sea. Micah 7:18-19

And forgive us our debts, as we forgive our debtors. Matthew 6:12

For if ye forgive men their trespasses, your heavenly Father will also forgive you: But if ye forgive not men their trespasses, neither will your Father forgive your trespasses. Matthew 6:14-15

In whom we have redemption through his blood, the forgiveness of sins, according to the riches of his grace. Ephesians 1:7

For I will be merciful to their unrighteousness, and their sins and their iniquities will I remember no more. Hebrews 8:12

But this man, after he had offered one sacrifice for sins for ever, sat down on the right hand of God. Hebrews 10:12

And their sins and iniquities will I remember no more. Now where remission of these is, there is no more offering for sin. Hebrews 10:17-18

If we confess our sins, he is faithful and just to forgive us our sins, and to cleanse us from all unrighteousness. 1 John 1:9

My little children, these things write I unto you, that ye sin not. And if any man sin, we have an advocate with the Father, Jesus Christ the righteous: And he is the propitiation for our sins: and not for ours only, but also for the sins of the whole world. 1 John 2:1-2

Thou shalt not avenge, nor bear any grudge against the children of thy people, but thou shalt love thy neighbour as thyself: I am the Lord. Leviticus 19:18

Therefore if thou bring thy gift to the altar, and there rememberest that thy brother hath ought against thee; Leave there thy gift before the altar, and go thy way; first be reconciled to thy brother, and then come and offer thy gift. Matthew 5:23-24

But I say unto you, Love your enemies, bless them that curse you, do good to them that hate you, and pray for them which despitefully use you, and persecute you. Matthew 5:44

And forgive us our debts, as we forgive our debtors. Matthew 6:12

For if ye forgive men their trespasses, your heavenly Father will also forgive you: But if ye forgive not men their trespasses, neither will your Father forgive your trespasses. Matthew 6:14-15

Then came Peter to him, and said, Lord, how oft shall my brother sin against me, and I forgive him? till seven times? Jesus saith unto him, I say not unto thee, Until seven times: but, Until seventy times seven. Matthew 18:21-22

Judge not, and ye shall not be judged: condemn not, and ye shall not be condemned: forgive, and ye shall be forgiven. Luke 6:37

Whose soever sins ye remit, they are remitted unto them; and whose soever sins ye retain, they are retained. John 20:23

To whom ye forgive any thing, I forgive also: for if I forgave any thing, to whom I forgave it, for your sakes forgave I it in the person of Christ lest satan should get an advantage of us: for we are not ignorant of his devices. 2 Corinthians 2:10-11

Let all bitterness, and wrath, and anger, and clamour, and evil speaking, be put away from you, with all malice: And be ye kind one to another, tenderhearted, forgiving one another, even as God for Christ's sake hath forgiven you. Ephesians 4:31-32

Grudge not one against another, brethren, lest ye be condemned: behold, the judge standeth before the door. James 5:9

Use hospitality one to another without grudging. 1 Peter 4:9

Forbearing one another, and forgiving one another, if any man have a quarrel against any: even as Christ forgave you, so also do ye. Colossians 3:13

Meditation Scriptures

PROMISES OF GOD

And take not the word of truth utterly out of my mouth; for I have hoped in thy judgments. Psalm 119:43

My tongue shall speak of thy word: for all thy commandments are righteousness. Psalm 119:172

We having the same spirit of faith, according as it is written, I believed, and therefore have I spoken; we also believe, and therefore speak. 2 Corinthians 4:13

Fight the good fight of faith, lay hold on eternal life, whereunto thou art also called, and hast professed a good profession before many witnesses. 1 Timothy 6:12

Seeing then that we have a great high priest, that is passed into the heavens, Jesus the Son of God, let us hold fast our profession. Hebrews 4:14

Let us hold fast the profession of our faith without wavering; for he is faithful that promised. Hebrews 10:23

But what saith it? The word is nigh thee, even in thy mouth, and in thy heart: that is, the word of faith, which we preach. Romans 10:8

Say unto them, As truly as I live, saith the Lord, as ye have spoken in mine ears, so will I do to you. Numbers 14:28

But that on the good ground are they, which in an honest and good heart, having heard the word, keep it, and bring forth fruit with patience. Luke 8:15

For whatsoever things were written aforetime were written for our learning, that we through patience and comfort of the scriptures might have hope. Romans 15:4

And let us not be weary in well doing: for in due season we shall reap, if we faint not. Galatians 6:9

For all the promises of God in him are yea, and in him Amen, unto the glory of God by us. 2 Corinthians 1:20

That ye be not slothful, but followers of them who through faith and patience inherit the promises. Hebrews 6:12

And so, after he had patiently endured, he obtained the promise. Hebrews 6:15

Cast not away therefore your confidence, which hath great recompence of reward. For ye have need of patience, that, after ye have done the will of God, ye might receive the promise. For yet a little while, and he that shall come will come, and will not tarry. Hebrews 10:35-37

Who through faith subdued kingdoms, wrought righteousness, obtained promises, stopped the mouths of lions. Hebrews 11:33

But let him ask in faith, nothing wavering. For he that wavereth is like a wave of the sea driven with the wind and tossed. For let not that man think that he shall receive any thing of the Lord. A double minded man is unstable in all his ways. James 1:6-8

And Jesus answering saith unto them, Have faith in God. For verily I say unto you, That whosoever shall say unto this mountain, Be thou removed, and be thou cast into the sea; and shall not doubt in his heart, but shall believe that those things which he saith shall come to pass; he shall have whatsoever he saith. Therefore I say unto you, What things soever ye desire, when ye pray, believe that ye receive them, and ye shall have them. Mark 11:22-24

He staggered not at the promise of God through unbelief; but was strong in faith, giving glory to God; Romans 4:20

Well; because of unbelief they were broken off, and thou standest by faith. Be not highminded, but fear. Romans 11:20

And he did not many mighty works there because of their unbelief. Matthew 13:58

Meditation Scriptures

CLEANSING OF THE WORD

Wherewithal shall a young man cleanse his way? by taking heed thereto according to thy word. Psalm 119:9

Seeing ye have purified your souls in obeying the truth through the Spirit unto unfeigned love of the brethren, see that ye love one another with a pure heart fervently. 1 Peter 1:22

Having therefore these promises, dearly beloved, let us cleanse ourselves from all filthiness of the flesh and spirit, perfecting holiness in the fear of God. 2 Corinthians 7:1

That he might sanctify and cleanse it with the washing of water by the word. Ephesians 5:26

The words of the Lord are pure words: as silver tried in a furnace of earth, purified seven times. Psalm 12:6

The statutes of the Lord are right, rejoicing the heart: the commandment of the Lord is pure, enlightening the eyes. Psalm 19:8

Thy word is a lamp unto my feet, and a light unto my path. Psalm 119:105

And now, brethren, I commend you to God, and to the word of his grace, which is able to build you up, and to give you an inheritance among all them which are sanctified. Acts 20:32